LIFE'S LITTLE GEMS

Edited by

Heather Killingray

First published in Great Britain in 2001 by
POETRY NOW
Remus House,
Coltsfoot Drive,
Peterborough, PE2 9JX
Telephone (01733) 898101
Fax (01733) 313524

HB ISBN 0 75432 608 X
SB ISBN 0 75432 609 8

FOREWORD

Although we are a nation of poets we are accused of not reading poetry, or buying poetry books. After many years of listening to the incessant gripes of poetry publishers, I can only assume that the books they publish, in general, are books that most people do not want to read.

Poetry should not be obscure, introverted, and as cryptic as a crossword puzzle: it is the poet's duty to reach out and embrace the world.

The world owes the poet nothing and we should not be expected to dig and delve into a rambling discourse searching for some inner meaning.

The reason we write poetry (and almost all of us do) is because we want to communicate: an ideal; an idea; or a specific feeling. Poetry is as essential in communication, as a letter; a radio; a telephone, and the main criterion for selecting the poems in this anthology is very simple: they communicate.

CONTENTS

BEYOND THE CRADLE

Unconditional love descends,
Divine in origin.
A glowing sphere of happiness
Envelops you within.
To this warm and precious issue
Your fond hand will attend.
This deepening adoration
Will never know an end.
Each and every move that's made
You will lovingly watch,
All the whimpering sounds
Invite your tender touch.

You'll nurture this priceless treasure,
As but a woman could.
The greatest of endowments is
The gift of motherhood.
As months and years pass swiftly by,
The babe becomes a man.
Many a sacrifice was made
To help things run to plan.
But freely of yourself you give,
And never count the cost,
Because, in all those trying times,
Your love is never lost.

Wherever this new person roams,
A part of you goes too.
The richest gift he'll ever have
Is that love giv'n by you.

Wendy R Thomas

BEDTIME PRAYERS

I hold my dolly tightly,
Then I wend my way upstairs . . .
Mummy comes to tuck me in
When I have said my prayers.

I kneel beside my little bed,
Then close my eyes and pray.
I thank God for my parents
Whom I love more each day.

I thank God for bright rainbows,
Moonbeams, stars and shining sun
Which beams down on my garden
Where I like to skip and run!

I ask Him to bless my friends,
My cat and puppy too!
We have such fun together
And find lots of things to do!

Mummy comes to say, 'Good night.'
And I close my sleepy eyes . . .
May holy angels guard me
Until the morning skies . . .

D Townshend

CHERISHED LOVE

My love's sailed away
        across the sea
The sincerest of love
        sailed away from me -
But their flag-ship returns
        with each new day
A telepathic compass
        they call to say -
'We love you Nanny'.

And I feel their hugs
        as their hearts cry out -
For the simple love
        they want to shout it out,
With hugs and kisses from
        across the sea -
How dearly I treasure
        their thoughts for me.

And in this simple way
        no money can buy,
Such love is spread -
        it is given free,
And each heart that beats
        across the sea -
In my own heart I cherish
        their love for me.

Mary Skelton

MOTHER AND SON

I used to take you in my arms
And kiss your tears away
When you were hurt you ran to me
But that was yesterday.

When you were a little boy
And all my very own
Now you are a man
And you must learn to stand alone.

But sometimes when I see that
There are troubles on your mind
I long to bear your burdens
And wish that I could find.

A way to show my love to you
But what help can I be
The years have passed and you have
Grown beyond your need of me.

D Sheasby

SON

I remember the day that you were born,
It was a cold and frosty morn,
Grass, glowing like crystal,
Spiked by the sun.
As I gazed out of the window
We have a son.
I turned my eyes to see you there
A tiny baby in my care,
For now and always
I'll love you so
My little one, our only son.

Doreen Ellen Thomson

MOTHERHOOD

Their future waits them,
Who knows what it may hold?

I give them bricks and mortar,
Try to be a firm foundation.
Always torn between them
Having it all, and only what is good.

Offer them protection
While breeding independence,
A confusing contradiction.

Knowing, always knowing
That awful time is coming,
The moment of their going.

Joyce Walker

A NEW BABY

At last my little bump
I've been nurturing since conception
Is about to be born.
I've felt it kicking,
I've seen pictures of it on the scan,
So I know it's definitely there!

The birth was more painful than expected,
Taking as much energy as a marathon run,
But now my little bundle is here in my arms,
The job of parenting has only just begun!

It's a hard job being a mum -
Frequently exhausted,
Deprived of sleep,
Little time for myself in those early days.
I must make the most of this time, though,
'Bonding' is the word . . .
As I look at his lovely little face
And he gazes up at me.
I'm learning to understand his needs . . .
Hungry, wet nappy,
Nappy change urgent,
Tired, colic or wind.

But the rewards are immeasurable -
To think we have produced a little person
Who will grow up to be a man.
I'm sure he will make a special contribution
To our world - this child with such potential!

Cathy Mearman

SWEET MOTHERHOOD
(To my darling baby girls, Maria and Jade)

I dreamed and dreamed for many years
Sweet wishes, washed with crystal tears
That God would speed, from up above
The dearest babe, for me to love.

For years and years, my dream was not
What had I done to be forgot
To be denied this precious dream
Inside, my lonely soul would scream.

So many questions in my mind
The answers, I could never find
I had been wronged, I had no voice
The mighty Lord had made this choice.

I'd give my heart and all I bear
To nurture all my tender care
Unto the child my soul yearns for
To wash upon my barren shore.

This candle in my heart burns so
And nobody will ever know
This yearning tears me inside out
This pain, it wracks my heart throughout.

Then just as hope was out of sight
The Lord shone down a blinding light
He blessed me with a child of mine
A precious girl, a gift divine.

My miracle now's shared in two
As heaven sent a sister too
Both beautiful in sight and soul
Sweet motherhood, my cherished goal.

Always the centre of my world
My precious, baby darling girls
This special love we share together
Will keep us close, always, forever.

All my love
Mummy.

Maxine Godfrey

LITTLE ONES

A baby enters this world of ours,
And we are very grateful as we learn much from their small powers.
Over the years they learn the right things to do,
And when guided well their bright lights come smiling through.
All can have a nasty little tantrum,
But if given in to - life becomes quite hum-drum.
Youngsters look to elders for advice,
And to be ready to help them always proves very nice.
We can only suggest things as they grow in years,
But a quiet word will allay many fears.
Children's greatest wish is to please all around -
And they will willingly do this if they are safe and sound.
All children wish to do is fill you with pride,
So forgive mistakes readily, it makes for a smoother ride.
One of the biggest lessons they'll ever learn,
Is how work they should never spurn.
By mixing work with pleasure,
They could become a real little treasure.

Betty Green

A NEW LIFE

Beautiful blue eyes, hair of fine gold,
Sweet is the face of this baby I hold.
Asleep she's an angel, innocent and pure,
She fills me with pride so much that I'm sure
This heart of mine will burst at the seam,
As I gaze down in wonder at this vision, this dream.
Gaiety and laughter fills each corner of the house,
This baby now a toddler, isn't quiet as a mouse,
She's boisterous and noisy, a demon at times,
But in the next breath, she's serene and sublime.
Her toddler days over, we begin teenage years,
And in-between laughter we shed a few tears.
She's growing up fast now her make-believe days,
Are turning so quickly into adult ways,
Together we've grown and taken life stage by stage,
I turn around and find she has come to the age,
When the boy she has chosen wants her for his bride,
In her future a new threshold, the door is open wide,
Step through it my love, go as a healthy young wife,
And begin a new cycle, within you, a new life.

Rita M Arksey

WELCOME TO THE WORLD
(Evan Peter - 11.01.2001)

It was a holiday of a lifetime
For our 40th anniversary,
A trip to New Zealand while in our prime,
Alas, it was destined never to be.

Plans drawn and necessary bookings made,
In plenty of time for the year ahead,
New suitcases bought and deposits paid,
Choice made for a single or double bed.

All in place for this special holiday,
When out of the blue our daughter had news,
Expecting a baby January,
She happily asked us what were our views.

Our first grandchild was born, a bonny lad,
Both thought him best present we'd ever had.

Betty Mealand

WHO'D HAVE 'EM?

Kids can be a pleasure,
They can also be a pain,
They can send you round the twist,
Then turn you round again,
One minute you're in turmoil,
Then laughing like a clown,
Or crying in your coffee,
And hoping you don't drown,
But all the years of ups and downs,
Are worth their weight in gold,
For there's nothing quite so precious,
As your lovely kids to hold,
So let's all raise our glasses,
For the miracle of birth,
And send thanks to our God above,
'Cos he knows what they're worth.

Corinne Tuck

TREASURE

When you were in your cradle
My heart just flowed with love,
So sweet, so soft, and very new.
A gift from God above,
            Precious treasure.

Soon you were toddling round me,
Searching for books and for toys,
Laughing and running about the house,
A bundle of laughter and noise.
            Mummy's treasure.

Then oh, so quickly came schooldays,
You looked so grown-up that day,
A lorry came rumbling down the road,
And we were both in the way.
            Lost treasure.

Removing dust and bric-brac, spring cleaning
There they were - pink satin shoes.
Neatly wrapped in soft tissue
So nostalgic, so gold a hue -
            Memories treasured.

Peggy Briston

MY WORLD

I remember your first tiny steps,
A milestone - so it seemed,
Your teenage years, your doubts and fears
Wrapped up in hopes and dreams.

I taught you manners, right from wrong
I taught you how to smile
And when the day drew to a close -
I cuddled you the while.

I had you such a short time
For you were only lent
'Til you gave your heart to another -
But you still were heaven-sent.

And through the troubles and the strife
I would not change one thing,
For I've known the sweetness and delight
That children always bring.

Now in the twilight of my years
I look back and I see
How much a mother's love can shape
A life - a destiny.

Patricia Whiting

NEW BABE

Oh little child do not weep
Just open your eyes and take a peep
Can you not see you are safe and sound
With all of your family close around
Oh little one do not fret
For you are everyone's little pet
Let us see that pretty smile
And those gentle charms us beguile
Oh little one do not cry
Do not ask the reason why
Just know that you are very dear
And to our hearts you bring good cheer
Let all your days be sunny and bright
Let angels watch over you every night
And may you always safely be
Warm in the love of your family.

Margaret Gurney

TO THE DREAMER'S CHILD

Though folded their tents and put away
Their dreams still ferment in me today,
And in my dreaming and my singing
Becomes much clearer, nearer, as I go
Ever upwards winging.

I would have you not forget their songs,
But dream the dream which still belongs
To them, and children of their getting -
That setting suns shall rise,
Summers be eternal, under wide blue skies!

Dan Pugh

MOTHER LOVE

A look that dwells in wonder seeks
the words a loving mother speaks,
Little arms a neck enfold
as whispered takes of fun unfold,
Those eyes that say I love you Mum
when time for sleep has come,
The sandman comes and bids you sleep
perchance - that elfin smile to keep.

Edmund Hyde

TORN

When I was one and you were two
  Mum was always looking blue -
Dad decided they'd get through
  And cheered her up no end

By saying we would soon grow up
  Be easier and not young pups -
But he was wrong and before long
  We drove him round the bend

But funny now we're far away
  You posted out the other day -
Me going off to France in May -
  Dad asked me could he lend

Those teddies he gave you and me
  Round about when we were three -
He says he wants to just go see
  If they're too torn to mend

Now Dad's no sentimental kind
  Says Mum and him's got half a mind -
To fix old left arounds he finds
  Now he's got time to spend

So when we come home from the war
  Our teddies will be like before
He loves us, Jim, I can't write more
  Dad's cursing me again.

Peter Asher

TINY FEET

Mice in the pantry
Mice on the stair
Everywhere you look
Mice everywhere.

Shoo'sh listen
To the patter of tiny feet
Running stealthily
Through the street,
Busy with their chores
Do they worry
About locked doors?
Through the tiny holes
They creep
With their tiny feet.

Mice in the pantry
Mice on the stair
Everywhere you look
Mice everywhere.

The trap is set
But they are wise
Not to go too close -
Do they surmise
How the cheese is caught
And not the mouse?
Leaves a question
To be thought.

Mice in the pantry
Mice on the stair
Everywhere you look
Mice everywhere.

Beverley Beck

COUNT YOUR BODY

I have 1 head to nod at you,
I have 2 eyes to see you too
I have 2 ears to hear everything
And I have 1 mouth so I can sing.

I have 1 nose so I can smell,
And 1 tongue to talk and tell,
I have 2 lips to give you a peck,
And underneath that I have 1 neck.

I have 2 arms to stretch up tall,
And I have 2 hands to catch a ball,
I have 2 legs so I can run,
And 2 feet to jump up and have fun.

You have 10 of something what can they be?
Look at your body and you will see,
It's not your mouth and it's not your nose,
Yes it's 10 fingers and also 10 toes!

J D Mead

SNOW PEOPLE

Hey My Snowman, where did you go?
I gave you a name and called you Joe.
Hey Mrs Snowman, no need to pout,
It will get better, the sun's coming out.
Hey Mrs Snowman, no need to wane,
It's only a little shower of rain!
Hey Mrs Snowman, no need to go
See you next year, when it starts to snow!

Margaret Bajai

BETSY

I know a monster,
It lives under the stairs,
I think its name is Betsy,
It has lots and lots of hairs.

It has four big round eyes,
And its skin is really sticky.
Its belly is as green as bogeys,
Urrgh, how icky!

Betsy is a friendly monster,
Whose favourite drink is milk.
Betsy has a pretty dress,
She says it's made of silk.

Betsy has sausages for tea,
Covered all over with glue.
I am Betsy's best friend,
Will you be Betsy's friend too?

Zack Gardener

THE OLD LAMP LIGHTER

How everyone takes things for granted
these days,
like walking down a darkened road,
and suddenly seeing all the lights
come on along the highways
without the raising of a hand,
or the flicker of a flame.
When I was a little girl, there wasn't any
electricity in the streets or lanes,
we had gas lamps, children used to watch,
as a man walked up and down the streets.
He carried a long thin rod, with a hook
on the end,
and when he reached a lamp,
he'd put the hook on the rod,
into the loop on the lamp, and pull,
then the light would go on,
he was known as the 'lamp lighter'.
After the lamp lighter had gone
children would play in the lamp light
until it was time for bed.
In the morning the lamp lighter
would return and put them out.

Peggy Johnson

SOPHIE

Sophie, my little girl
Likes to dance and likes to twirl
She is full of mischief, full of fun
And likes to play outside in the sun
She can sing all the high notes but not the low
She can run very fast she is never slow
She can climb a mountain, scramble over rocks
She doesn't wear shoes, not even socks
I like to see her play at leap frog
Because I am proud of my little dog.

Jean-Ruth

WHERE IS HE NOW?

He is gone, I know not where
Gone and vanished in the air
Hanging on an unseen thread
Ever dangling overhead
Travelling where he wants to go
And I'm sure that I don't know
I just saw him he was gone
Very early in the morn
He hid not shout or make a sound
So very high above the ground
Just a black speck in the air
Travelling, moving everywhere
He has gone I know not where
Gone to spin another home
Has his work to do
That lovely great big spider might
       pay a call on you.

George Camp

ANIMALS

A long time ago a wise man named Noah.
Saved all of the animals, all the world over.

Some of the animals we see at the zoo
The elephant, zebra, kangaroo.

Some of the animals that live in a house
Puppy, kitten, little mouse.

Some of the animals that live near water
The beaver, water rat, otter.

Some of the animals that climb a tree
Squirrel, pine marten, chimpanzee.

Some animals that live in a hole
Badger, rabbit, mole.

Some animals that don't mind the snow
Polar bear, reindeer and buffalo.

Some of the animals the farmers keep
Horses, pigs, cows and sheep.

Anne Haire

TWO YEARS OLD

I'm two years old and not very bold
My mummy tells me 'to do as I'm told'
But it's really hard 'cause I'm not very old.

My brother and sister are really big
They dress me up and give me a wig
They put on lipstick and tell my mum
She looks at me and says, 'What have you done!'

I go to toddlers to see my friends
We play hide and seek and make lots of dens
Mummy chats to all the mums
Non-stop chatter about their big fat tums
We have cake and squash and make lots of mess
Mum says, 'Look at you and your brand new dress!'

We go to the shop to buy some sweets
Mummy says, '*Stop,* that's enough treats.'
I stamp my feet hard, it really hurts
So much so, I fell off the kerb
My mummy now is very *cross*
She picks me up and says, *'I'm the boss!'*

Mummy and Daddy cuddle me lots
Even when I have chicken pox
They say they love me no matter what
I know that's true cause we're all they've got

I'm one big bundle of humorous fun
I'm not that naughty when all's said and done!
I'm only two
And I'm just for you. XX

Julie Khan

MAKING SPELLS

Mrs Witch is fat and happy
She is seldom snappy.
She has six pixie workers
And none of them are shirkers,
But the purple pixie who is fond of treacle pud
Always finds it hard to be good.
Now by the house of Mrs Witch
A blue tree stands
With no leaves
But little hands
Ready to grab you,
But it only grabs bad little pixies
Especially if they are wearing purple bells.
Inside the kitchen
A magic pot hangs
Upon the wall,
Until Mrs Witch yells
Come on my pixie friends, let's have a ball
Making the most fantastic spells.
Bring me tea pot dregs,
From spiders, a dozen hairy legs
And from worms the most wriggly ends.
Dump them all in my magic pot
And stir, stir, stir the lot.
There were some smoky flashes,
A shower of violet ashes
Followed by a series of mighty bangs,
And now the witch in the blue tree hangs.

Pat Isiorho

In The Wood

'Tis said there lives in yonder wood,
A witch by name of Ghool,
And as you pass by her old hut,
Behold her on her stool.

Around her sit a dozen cats,
Or so the people say,
And in her lap there rests a book,
Which she reads day by day.

The book is full of magic spells,
That she weaves all day long,
And as you pass by you will hear,
Her singing her weird song.

Of her the people liked to speak,
To strangers as they came,
But in their own hearts they did think,
That she was all too tame.

For only rumours spoke of spells,
That she had put on folk,
And after all they might you know,
Be only just a joke.

Pauline Dodworth

THE ALPHABET

A is for *adventure*, scrambling and tumbling.
B is for *bee*, buzzing and bumbling.
C is for *cat*, sly as can be.
D is for *dad*, who always burns my tea.
E is for *everyone*, living together.
F is for *friends*, for being pals forever.
G is for *giant*, big and mean.
H is for *helpful*, kind and keen.
I is for *inviting* people to your party.
J is for *joking*, acting like a smarty.
K is for *kite*, flying in the sky.
L is for *lion*, roaring when you pass by.
M is for *Mummy*, she's gentle, I'll bet.
N is for *nappies* that babies get wet!
O is for *orange*, a colour that's bright.
P is for *pigs* - what a sight!
Q is for *queen*, who always looks fine.
R is for *river*, like the Tyne.
S is for *sun*, *sea* and *sand*.
T is for *toys*, broken by your hand.
U is for *unicorn*, riding in the wood.
V is for *victory*, winning like you should.
W is for *weather*, come sun or snow.
X is for *xylophone*, notes high and low.
Y is for *yodel*, screaming very loud.
Z is for *zebra*, walking very proud.
You may not know it yet,
But you'll soon learn your *alphabet*!

Indi Anna Jones (12)

GRAN-MA

Gran-ma, Gran-ma,
Sing a song or two,
Sing a song so
We want to be with you.

Gran-ma, Gran-ma,
Bake a cake or two,
You bake them like no one
else bakes them at all.

Gran-ma, Gran-ma,
Show me how to stitch,
And with those special sticks,
Show me how to knit.

Gran-ma, Gran-ma,
Now that you are 85,
I wish I can be with you,
From 9 to 5.

A Bhambra

THE BLACK CAT

There was once a very black cat,
Who had a great big blue mat,
He sat on it night and morning,
And never moved to say hello,
When it came to dawning.

But little did I know,
He went out on the town
With the ginger cat, Moe,
Mind you in the morning,
He always came back yawning.

That black cat of mine,
Was all over very fine,
But I ask in delight,
'Do you know what your cat does at night?'

Anneka Ranken (13)

LITTLE BOY LOST

The little swing is still.
The little boy is gone.
The fall of autumn leaves goes on and on
and on.
The moon is very pale.
A late bird song is sad.
Soon the night will come
and bats will fly.
I feel a cool little hand in mine.
I see a little fair head and
trusting blue eyes.
I wonder where that little boy has gone?
Gone so far away from me.
The owl calls a lonely cry.
There is no answer for me in the
lonely night.

Jennifer M Trodd

ALL GOD'S CHILDREN

'What do you want for Christmas, my super-intelligent pet?'
'I want a new computer, and I want to surf the net
And I want a personal mobile
And a brand new snorkelling set.'

'What do you want for Christmas, my precious darling child?'
'I want to go to Lapland, where the snow is thick and piled,
And to meet with Father Christmas
And the reindeer in the wild.'

'What would you like for Christmas, little Janey and Peter and Paul?'
'A puppy, a doll and a teddy bear, and a bat and a bouncy ball,
And some lollipops and chocolates
And some soldiers straight and tall.'

'What would you like at Christmas, dear children who have no home?'
'We'd like a mother to love us, and a hut to call our own;
And some bread, and water that's pure and clean,
And never again to roam.'

'What will do at Christmas, youngsters of many treats?
Will you save some coins and offer a prayer for kids on the cold
dark streets,
For the refugees and the hurting ones
With injured arms and feet?'

'What will you give at Christmas, Oh children of God above?
Will you give of yourselves and your gifts from Him who leads you
with reins of love?
Will you help your mums, and thank your dads
And your Father of love above?'

Nancie Cator

THE CATERPILLAR'S CHATTER

Would it matter if the chatter,
That came from the caterpillar,
Made not a bit of sense to you and me?
Would we notice one jot, if he forgot
To sound his Ps' and Qs' whilst out to tea?
If he stuttered would we mutter,
Would we really mind at all,
If his words were absurd,
And we thought him quite a nerd.
Do you think that we would take the time to tell?
I think that I would rather,
If it's all the same to you,
Admire the way he quietly moves around.
With so many feet, it's astounding that he moves
After mastering the walking,
There is just no time for talking,
He really has got nothing left to prove.
So would it matter, that the chatter,
That came from the caterpillar
Made not one jot of sense at all?
Why of course not, I clean forgot,
They don't talk, not caterpillars,
        They just crawl!

Caren Jayne

THE LITTLE CAT

There was a little cat
And his name was Sam.
His fur was black with a little bit of white
And he liked to go out hunting in the middle of the night.

He didn't mind the dark:
His eyes were like two lamps.
He loved to chase the little mice,
Who ran away from him in a trice.

One day Sam found a lovely pond
Full of brightly coloured fish
He badly wanted to catch a big one,
But couldn't think how it could be done.

Sam stretched out a paw;
He was too far away.
He leant a bit farther and fell in with a plop.
Oh dear, what has happened - I just couldn't stop!

Now Sam's decided that fishing's no good
And he's had enough of that rather wet sport.
He prefers to go out when it's quiet and dark,
To chase mice and whatever else might be there in the park.

Mary Capurro

SKIPPING RHYME

Watch for the postman!
  Here he comes.
Open the letters,
  Fingers and thumbs.

Watch for the milkman!
  Hear his horse.
Ice-cold bottles
  And cream, of course.

Watch for the dustman!
  Lift up the bins,
Empty them out -
  Boxes and tins.

I Keatinge

THE ANIMAL ALPHABET

A is for *alligator*, snappy and bad,
B is for *bear*, all chained up and sad.

C is for *cats*, who run very fast,
D is for *donkey* or is it an ass?

E is for *elephant* so large and so grey,
F is for *fish*, the whale's prey.

G is for *giraffe*, so slim and so tall,
H is *hawk* with an eye on us all.

I is for *iguana*, all scaly and still,
J is for *jackal*, who's out for the kill.

K is for *kangaroo*, who packs a punch,
L is for *lion* on the lookout for lunch.

M is for *monkey*, who swings in the tree,
N is for *narwhal*, the beast of the sea.

O is for *ostrich*, who lays giant-sized eggs,
P is for *panda* with short stubby legs.

Q is for *quail*, so pretty and nice,
R is for *rats*, who bully the mice.

S is for *snake*, it is seen but not heard,
T is for *toucan*, a big-billed bird.

U is for *urchins*, they're one of a kind,
V is for *vole*, helpless and blind.

W is for *whale*, the star of the show,
X is for nothing, as we all know!

Y is for *yak*, who's so hairy and wild,
Z is for *zoo*, where you can take your child.

Jonathan Norman (12)

THE GOBBLER

Don't upset the Gobbler, he might just eat you up,
And if you make a drink for him, don't make it in a cup,
Make it in a bucket, and fill it to the top,
Leave it quite close to him, and stand by with a mop,
The Gobbler is a clumsy creature, he might spill some on the floor,
So if he's feeling thirsty, give him a large straw,
Don't upset the Gobbler, he might jump on your head,
And if he's still fast asleep, don't go near his bed,
Don't wake up the Gobbler, it's not a pretty sight,
His big red eyes will stare at you, and he'll want to have a fight,
So if your friends are with you, and you're playing with some toys,
Make sure that you play quietly, and don't make any noise,
Don't upset the Gobbler, you might make him stamp and roar,
And if he starts to chase you, run out through the door,
If the Gobbler is feeling hungry, never ever tease,
He will snatch you by your legs, and nibble on your knees,
So if his tummy is rumbling, then give him lots to eat,
The Gobbler loves tyres and chips, as a special treat,
If the Gobbler seems quite happy, and hasn't got the blues,
Play a simple game with him, but *never* let him lose,
Because if the Gobbler gets upset, and thinks that he may not win,
He will chew your game into little pieces, and spit them in the bin,
Then with his furry fingers, he will grab you by the hair,
And lifting you up at least ten feet, will throw you through the air,
It's true to say that the Gobbler, is a most unusual pet,
Eight feet tall with purple fur, how much stranger could he get?
But if you keep him happy, and on you he can depend,
The Gobbler will be nice to you, and be your special friend . . .

Stephen Norris

FIREWORK NIGHT

We sat in the greenhouse to watch the fun,
Dad lit the fireworks one by one,
The rockets went off with a swoosh and a bang,
The noise in our ears just boomed and rang.

Cascades, fountains and golden rain,
With Catherine wheels again and again,
Sparklers in hand and a Christmas tree,
What a glorious sight for us to see.

When we all went in to have our tea,
What a lovely feast we there did see,
Hot soup, hot dogs, potatoes too,
Popcorn and cakes for me and you.

Thank you for fun on firework night,
Thank you for such a splendid sight,
Thank you for all we see and do,
To Mummy and Daddy, a big thank you.

Mary Stace

THE RAINBOW

Look through the window, there's a rainbow in the sky
Raindrops and puddles mean there is no outdoor play.
With books and paints sit to the table and keep dry,
Draw and paint the rainbow it will soon fade away.

Mary E Beale

THE FLOODING SEA

Do not rock us
Do not sway,
Let us fish
Another day.

All we have is sails
And rope
We catch the tide
On poor mariner's hope.

The sky is dark
The sea is grey,
Our boat shall sink
Or so they say

We cannot return
Without any fish,
Our families are waiting
A most tasty dish!

The children wait eagerly
Around the port,
To hear of our tales
Of what we have caught

The tables are set
The fires are burning,
Leave us afloat
While the tide is turning.

So, do not rock us
Do not sway!
Let us fish
Another day!

S P Springthorpe

A To Z

A,B,C,D,E,
Look how easy it can be.

F,G,H,I,J,
You can learn some everyday.

K,L,M,N,O,
Halfway there, come on let's go.

P,Q,R,S,T,
You'll finish if you follow me.

U,V,W,X,Y,
It's almost time to say goodbye.

Last comes Z,
Now cuddle up with Ted,
Because it's time to go to bed.

Emily Pool

SCRUFFY BEAR

I have a little teddy bear
Who doesn't like to comb his hair
He never seems to wash his clothes
Brush his teeth or wipe his nose

All he ever wants to do
Is stuff himself with dumpling stew
Or fill his huge round furry tummy
With loads and loads of bread and honey

Can you imagine the mess he makes
Eating chocolate covered cakes
Sandwiches filled with mustard ham
And jars of sticky strawberry jam?

Sadly I must confess
My little teddy looked a mess
The only way to get him clean
Was to pop him in the washing machine

I watched poor teddy going round
Making a muffled gurgling sound
With bubbles in-between his toes
Behind his ears and up his nose

The washing machine made a terrible din
During the final 'super spin'
I pulled him out - but he was fine
So I pegged him on the washing line.

Eileen Bailey

THE WIND

The cones on the trees
Look like little chicks all huddled together
Sheltering against the windy weather
Which is gale force at times
Rattling the windowpanes
Roaring down the chimney pots
Sounding as if it is raging and in pain
Whistling round the houses
Screaming through the locks.

'Let me in, let me in,' he cries
Or I shall smash all the crocks . . .

Now it has died down, all is still
The birds are silent in their nests till
Sleep cometh and all creatures rest
Until the break of day.

Gwyneth E Scott

Butterfly, Ladybird And Cuckoo

Butterflies flutter in the sun,
and look a pretty sight.
They come in many colours,
and some of them are white.
But when you try to catch one,
they just fly away.
Onto another flower,
because they don't want to play.

Ladybirds are red, and yellow,
with black spots on their back.
They are a kind of beetle,
and can fly with wings of black.
But when you try to touch one,
they don't fly away.
You can pick them up and hold them.
But they won't want to play.

Cuckoos call from a distant tree,
when they stop to rest.
But you will never find,
a cuckoo on a nest.
They call as they fly,
calling loud and clear.
'Cuckoo - cuckoo - cuckoo,'
in the country, every year.

Martin Snowdon

MR BIDDLE

Do you know Mr Biddle
who lives in the house in the middle,
not too far left, not too far right,
just in the middle, yellow and bright?
he's lived there all his life
with three sons and a wife;
The one in the middle
looks like Mr Biddle.
When they walk in the street,
Mr Biddle and the son in the middle,
they like to stamp their feet
and to walk in the middle,
not too far left, not too far right,
just in the middle, cheerful and bright.

Licia Johnston

MY DREAM CAR

At night my bed becomes a car
And takes me high above the stars.
Over the moon so silvery bright
To the place where day is night.
I drift along the Milky Way
And watch the moonbeams dance and play
I follow the trail of their silver beams
Which lead me to the Land of Dreams.

I don't need wheels to get me there
Just a cosy quilt and my teddy bear
No brakes, or engine on my bed
But a nice soft pillow for my head.
My little car just seems to know
Exactly where I want to go.
Up where colours light the sky
And shooting stars go whizzing by.

I wish my mum could come with me
And see the lovely things I see,
But when I told her where I'd been
She smiled and said, 'It's just a dream!'
But I know she's been there before
I found some moondust on her floor!

Elizabeth Mary McNally

ANIMALS

An ant is small,
A giraffe is tall,
A turtle has a shell,
An elephant remembers well.

A mouse squeaks,
An antelope leaps,
A snake will slither,
And a penguin may shiver.

A frog is green,
A lion is mean,
Elephants are grey,
Owls don't come out during the day.

Geraldine Watson

THE MAGIC TOY BOX

It's bed time for Toby,
The toys are put away,
In the wooden toy box,
Until another day.

When the house is sleeping,
And all is calm and still,
Those toys in that toy box
Jump out! They're never still.

There's cars and drums and trains,
And Barbie dolls galore,
Dancing round the play room,
Not anyone's a bore.

No one ever guesses,
The fun they have all night,
Until dawn comes calling,
And sunshine gleaming bright.

Back into the toy box,
They've really had a ball,
Cars, trains and Barbie dolls,
And Teddy, king of all.

Ivy Allpress

BENGIE TABBY CAT'S WORRYING DILEMMA

Bengie thought his mother Tabatha, must be terribly ill
She hadn't moved from her basket, she lay there oh so still
She was usually very active, rushing around doing this and that
But lately she was always tired and had become very fat

Bengie now was troubled and decided at home he would stay
But his father Toby reassured him, that everything was okay
He'd visit cousin Rupert Black Cat, he'd know what to do
Telling him of his mother's plight, he sat to think it through

There was only one thing for it, they'd have to visit the vet
Neither of them had any money, so they'd both end up in debt
Bengie thought it was hopeless, as tears filled in his eyes
They decided to find Felix Stitch-ear, he was old and very wise

Bengie became frightened, he feared the grumpy old cat
Looking so scarred and war-torn, after viciously fighting a rat
Felix lived at the vet's house and was sitting by the wall
The largest cat Bengie had seen, made him feel so small

Felix said the vet was out, he was visiting a sick horse
On hearing Bengie's dilemma, he said nature would take its course
Bengie couldn't settle and decided he would go home
He didn't feel like playing, he just wanted to be alone

Back home at the hardware store, a commotion was going on
Rushing to his mother's side, he wondered what was wrong
His father so proud to greet him, his eyes were full of glee
Tabatha had not only had one kitten, suddenly there was three

Bengie was delighted as he watched the bundles of fur
He felt so relieved and happy, to hear his mother purr
He couldn't hide his emotion, he couldn't help but cry
Hugging his mother, he told her, he thought she was going to die

Tabatha cuddled her son, saying everything would be just fine
They would now be a happy family, for a very very long time.

Linda Brown

MY DAD

My dad, he's my best mate
He never forgets or makes me late
He's big and strong
And can do no wrong
He's such fun
He's my best chum

We run and play
Almost every day
Sometimes we fight
With all our might
But that's just pretend
Because he's my best friend

We play hide and seek
And I try not to peak
I jump in puddles
And have lots of cuddles
Everything's great
With Dad, my best mate

Alexandra Ayton

WHAT IS A LIBRARY?

It could be *your* books that you have found
in charity shops for under a pound.

Presents from family, presents from friends,
standing between your Disney book-ends.

Or a roomful of books - two thousand or more
stacked on shelving from ceiling to floor.

Such magical stories there are on those shelves
of wizards and witches, the Hobbit and elves.

Robin Hood, secret gardens, dragons breathing fire,
knights of King Arthur serving their sire.

Read about fish, sharks with big jaws
or scary tales of extinct dinosaurs.

Racing cars, ships, railways and planes,
or characters called Borrowers hiding in drains.

Beatrix Potter animals, neat and small,
or the BFG who is strong and tall.

Space ships and aliens, rockets to stars,
frightening monsters, exciting Star Wars.

Stories of treasure, time-travel too,
animals who talk and those in a zoo.

So enter the library, it's an open door,
the world is yours, just come and explore.

Meet Long John Silver - find Narnia and Aslan
herd sheep with a pig - fly with Peter Pan
visit Chocolate Charlie - tame Pikachu
play Quidditch with Harry Potter - they're all waiting for you.

Yes, a library has books, that's what it seems
but never forget it also has dreams.

Anne Sansome

REACH FOR THE SUN

Oh, black and white and stripy 'Seed of a Sunflower'
Mummy tells me you hold a lot of power,
So I'm going to plant you in the soil
And promise to water you whilst you toil.

'It takes time' Mummy says 'til you'll show signs of life
You were so small when I buried you . . . I hope you're still alive.
But one morning Mummy shouted, 'Quick come outside!'
You'd broken through and, as I'd helped, I felt a feeling of pride!

Slowly, you keep growing
You surely seem to know where you're going!
Like your name you seem determined to reach for the sun
'Til one day you show your true beauty to everyone.

OK 'Big head'! Now you look down on me as well!
But, who knows? One day I might be as tall as you . . . Who can tell?

Carol Ann Kiddle

THE DISCO MIXER

As Tuffty mixed the music,
The disco came alive,
Sounds of the jungle filled the air,
Body's swaying, feet moving
to the steady bongo beat,
One could feel the tropical heat.

The talent of this young man,
Two records turning in unison,
Moving the rhythm from left to right,
Until the balance of the beat
filled the night.

He watched the dancer's faces,
They were smiling with delight,
Tuffty's hard work had not been in vain,
he would be asked to perform again,
Knowing that he had passed the test,
In the future Tuffty would be mixing
with the best.

Terri Brant

WATER BABY

Splashing
in a cool, blue pool
tiled with mosaic dolphins

Imagine
her ear-to-ear smile
while proud Granny looks on

Kicking
away from supporting hands,
bands of air-filled rubber are not for her

'Swim
to Granny' her mother says,
and who could miss the
option of a soggy kiss.

Catherine Bradbury

THE TOAD

The other day as I was walking down the road,
I slipped and fell over and bumped into Mr Toad.
I said, 'Hello Mr Toad, how are you,'
He said, 'How nice it is to see you too,'
Mr Toad looked up at me with his big eyes,
And started to speak to me he said, 'I have a surprise,'
As I turned round to him in shock,
I said to Mr Toad, 'How is Miss Stock?'
Miss Stock is a lovely rabbit with loads of white fur,
Mr Toad does not like Mrs Kit because she has a loud purr.
My name is Miss Daydream, I am a little dog,
Mr Toad and I get on well with Mr Frog.
Mr Toad said to me you know Miss Stock,
She ran off with her friend from round the block.
Mr Toad and I laughed with disbelief,
Mr Mouse was the rabbit with great big teeth.

Sally Warren

EYES

One day when the sky was grey and the pavements wet
Jonathan said to his auntie Bet,
'Make up a rhyme,'
'OK,' she said, 'this time,
It's all about eyes.'
'Eyes that are blue, eyes that are brown
Eyes that look up, eyes that look down.
Look up to the mountains, the moon and the stars,
Look this way and that, watch out for cars.
Use your eyes well.
The world is so full of things here and there,
Don't walk past them, stop and stare,
At a flower or a tree, or a cloud in the sky,
Or a boy who's wearing a bright red tie,
Or a girl in a lovely party dress.
Peep over that wall and can you guess
What's on the other side?
Some swings and a slide
When bedtime comes eyes closed for prayers and sleep,
And in the morning the sun will peep
In at the window as if to say
Come on, here's another day
Lots more lovely things to see,
Open your eyes and come with me.'

Elizabeth Bellis

A NOISY STORY - HARRIET HARE

Envious Harriet *hare*
Wanted to be a *bear*,
Eat honey without a *care*
Be messy *everywhere*.
But life was *so unfair*,
She at everyone did *glare*,
Face like a shrivelled *pear*
Others at her did *stare*.
So from this tale *beware*:
If you repeatedly *compare*
You'll look like Harriet *Hare*!

Gail

AMANDA MILLICENT MARY TRING

Amanda Millicent Mary Tring
Always knitted everything.
She'd started at the age of three
When, sat upon her granny's knee,
This somewhat solemn little girl
Learned first to *plain* and then to *purl.*

She quickly learned and soon was able
To knit in moss stitch, rib and cable.
She knitted scarves, she knitted hats
And striped socks for her granny's cats.
And for her brother's rabbit, Thumper,
She made a nice warm Fairisle jumper.

So by the time the summer came,
She was well into this knitting game!
For Father - a new deckchair cover,
A parasol to shelter Mother -
She knitted on for everyone
Her needles twinkling in the sun.

But when the family went away
To Wales, to take a holiday,
Amanda gasped in sheer surprise
For there, before her very eyes
Were sheep, with nothing on their backs!
Their coats were piled up in a sack!

'You poor things, you're turning blue,'
Said 'Manda, knowing what to do.
Out came her needles, and directly
She knitted blankets, one, two, three . . .
Until at last she'd made a heap
Of blankets, one for every sheep.

And there she got another shock!
For she could see a second flock
And then another, and another . . .
'I'll need more wool,' she said to Mother.
'I won't be long, I'm off to town
To get some cream, and black and brown,'

And she knitted rugs for every ewe,
For rams and lambs (and sheepdogs too).
But in the lumpy land of Wales
A trillion sheep graze in its dales,
So, for all I know, she is knitting still,
Just beyond that furthest hill!

Enid Middleton

EARLY MORNING SNACK

Footsteps on the landing
Creeping down the stairs
Feeling pangs of hunger
I reached for the bowl of pears
Sitting at the table
And munching away
Next thing I remembered
Was seeing light of day
Quietly going up the stairs
And getting into bed
Hoping to get back to sleep
When told 'Get up you sleepy head.'

Diana Daley

THE PHOTOGRAPH

The pale golden sand lay even like a
summer tablecloth as far as eye could see,
but, there it was a log half of a tree
nicely knurled sitting there above the
flat just like a golfer's tee.

Then Zoe with the flaming hair lay on
the warm trunk's top,
her mother took a snap, she wanted her
to let her shoes behind the log to flop.

They wandered in the sun,
the girl did not think birthday photographs
a lot of fun.

Some day she was to see how nice it all
could be,
as, she took photos of her girls that
she could show to me.

Jean Paisley

LIFE IS FULL OF SURPRISES

'Life is full of surprises,'
Said the ant to the great bumble bee.
'Take that spider who dropped from the ceiling,
And fell on Aunt Jessica's knee.'

'She jumped from her chair in a hurry,
We laughed as she called Aunty Nell,'
Who said, 'Don't shriek or act very silly,
Or Syd snail will come out of his shell.'

'Yes, that was a laugh,' said the beetle,
'But not quite so funny as when,
I tickled the toes of Aunt Lucy,
And she leapt on Great Uncle Ben.'

'Well I laugh the most,' said the blowfly
'For when Grandad is having a doze,
I know how to stop him from snoring,
I land on the bridge of his nose.'

Honor Riley

THE PIXIE AND THE FAIRY

Little Petal pixie
Flew with Flimsy fairy
Across the fields so far away
Upon a toadstool they did play

To dance on the toadstool so happily
Until, a gnome came down to see
He squashed the toadstool down
That naughty gnome who wore a frown

He spoilt their little game
They couldn't dance on the toadstool again
The elves came flying along
Singing a little song

They carried the gnome away
How Petal and Flimsy did play
Yet upon another toadstool
No more the gnome, could act the fool

Little Petal pixie and little Flimsy fairy
Were dancing with the elves so very happily
The gnomes was never heard of again
Never more to spoil their game.

Jean P McGovern

WHEN I WAS SMALL . . .

When I was small . . .

the days seemed to be so-o-o-o much longer!
the cream eggs seemed to be so-o-o-o much bigger!
the money seemed to go so-o-o-o much further!
the sun seemed to shine for so-o-o-o much longer!
the winters seemed to be so-o-o-o much frostier!
the snow seemed to fall and stay so-o-o-o much thicker!
the wild flowers seemed to be so-o-o-o much brighter!
the people seemed to be so-o-o-o much friendlier!
the pace of life seemed to be so-o-o-o much slower!
the steam train seemed to be so-o-o-o much nicer!
the buses seemed to be so-o-o-o much prompter!
the shop assistants seemed to be so-o-o-o much pleasanter!
the food seemed to be so-o-o-o much scrummier!
the adults seemed to be so-o-o-o much kinder!
the children seemed to be so-o-o-o much happier!
the beds seemed to be so-o-o-o much snugglier!
the coal fires seemed to be so-o-o-o much cosier!
the buildings seemed to be so-o-o-o much fewer!
the cars seemed to be so-o-o-o much slower!
the churches seemed to be so-o-o-o much fuller!
the views people had of life seemed to be so-o-o-o much clearer . . .
Didn't they?

Margi Hughes

GIPPY

Gippy was a toy giraffe
Given to me by Auntie Phoebe
When I was two and a half.
He went to bed with me
And even sat down to tea.
We had a great time together
At 'play' and always came
On Sundays 'for the walk'
To the woods.
Look Gippy, I would say that
Little squirrel up the oak tree
He has got a furry tail,
Not like yours which is 'smooth'.
We had such fun together.
In summer splashing about in the sea,
Getting wet,
You never complained,
Like my little brother,
I dropped Gippy from
The 'Dormobile' window,
Holding him out for fresh air
And I was never given another.

Marguerite A Auton

A SILLY VERSE

One, two I've lost my shoe
Three, four cats at the door
Five, six don't shout at the kids
Seven, eight oh please shut the gate
Nine, ten Mum's moaning again
Eleven, twelve put your books on the shelf
Thirteen, fourteen you're too young for courting
Fifteen, sixteen oh please don't tease the kitten
Seventeen, eighteen yes, we are all late again
Nineteen, twenty Joe don't kick that teddie
Twenty-one, twenty-two no you can't dye your hair blue
Twenty-three, twenty-four get out in the garden
                         and play with your ball
Twenty-five, twenty-six what's for lunch
                         oh we've got fish and chips
Twenty-seven, twenty-eight kids please don't argue,
                         I've got a headache
Twenty-nine, thirty where have you kids been
                         you're all filthy dirty.

Gillian Morrisey

FOOD FOR THOUGHT

Food for thought,
Where do you grow?
Where we do go,
The ground damp,
Autumn's here,
We haven't seen you yet,
You feed the soul,
Not knowing your goal
Upon a grassy knoll,
Fulfil my soul,
Fungus, food for thought.

K M Clemo

LET'S GO TO THE PARK

Now let's all go down to the park
And play exciting games
Like hide and seek, and hopscotch
And we'll have pretendy names
First the seesaw then the swings
And I'll push you to and fro
Then we'll all jump on the roundabout
And round and round we'll go.

Chorus

Now we'll take turns upon the slide
And see who's the fastest down
And swing across the climbing frame
The workmen brought from town
And then into the sandpit
And if we get bored, I know!
Once more on the roundabout
And round and round we'll go.

Chorus

Maybe we'll play some football
Or catch me if you can
But I would always win that
No matter how fast you ran
Or we'll play Mutant Turtles
And win all battles so
Then get back on the roundabout
And round and round we'll go

And round and round we'll go
And sing all the songs we know
And round and round we'll go,o,o,o
And round and round we'll go.

Don Woods

NEW SCOOTER

Can't it scoot Gran?
Yes it goes pell mell
But when you reach the lake
And forget your brake
There's no use ringing
The bell!
Splash!

Joan E Bartlett

STOP THE BUS
(A Belfast Game)

Throwing stones
At the bus
Faces staring
Back at us

Catapults
Increase their aim
Deadly simple
Is the game

Bricks and bottles
See them fly
Shattered glass
In someone's eye

Cause as much
Destruction to
The buses as they
Travel through

Hear the triumph
In their roar
Adding to
The bloody score

Children playing
On the street
Learn to feel
The battle's heat.

Kim Montia

THE WIND

Whistling, whining, swirling, spinning, turning, twisting, never still.
Blowing, gushing, madly rushing through the valley, o'er the hill.
Treetops quiver, washing shivers; small birds shelter where they may.
'Neath the hedges wild flowers tremble.
It's a *very* windy day!

Children chatter; small feet clatter on the pavement, as they run.
Faces smiling, looks beguiling; home from school, their work is done.
Rosy-cheeked from gales a-blowing, mothers put the washing away -
Dry as a bone and ready to iron.
It's a *very* windy day!

Margaret Tierney

UNTITLED

Incy Wincy spider's web
Spinning round the flower bed,
Clutching to the marigold,
Over the hedge and in the cold.

'Hello, Incy Wincy, dear'.
The crafty fly hoped he could hear.
His one eye up, the other down.
Incy Wincy did a frown.

Here was a fly, maybe from town,
Acting like a stupid clown.
Didn't he know the country law
Where flies were considered an absolute bore.

'Good morning, my tiny little friend'
Said Incy, slipping round the bend.
'I won't ask you into my parlour now
To have a cosy pow wow wow
But when the dawn creeps over the sky
And the dew is shimmering, glittering high,
Midget, feathery wings slip by
In dreamless weary sleep.
All too soon you'll be my guest
Lying on the cobweb's crest
Forever here to stay.'

'Oh do you think so, Incy dear
I really am not quite so sure
For sleep avoids me now, I fear.
When all around, the insects here
Peep out among the flowers near
The laurel hedge and lily pool
Keeping all the goldfish cool.
So - a busy little bee, I'll be
If you continue up the tree
Forgetting you ever saw me, me, me!'

Fly, however, did not know
That buried in the spider's brow
Were two sharp eyes which would perceive
His every move or motion - deed
Eleven legs and body round
Hasten to crush him to the ground.

Pauline Burton

MR TOAD

Mr Toad peeps out of his hole
On a bright and sunny day
He looks into the sky, and shouts
'Oh my, oh my!
What a great time I will have today.'

Mr Toad jumps into the pond,
Splashes around, and really
Makes quite a din
'Croak, croak,' he calls to his
Fishy friends
'Come with me, let's all go for
A swim.'

They swim around enjoying
Themselves
And really have so much fun
Then onto a rock he finally leaps
And dries himself in the hot sun.

Jaye Wood

CHERISH OUR CHILDREN

Children are the future, so show them that we care
Treat them all as equals, always try to be fair
When they grow up they'll be our best friend
If we show that we'll love them right till the end
There's nothing that we wouldn't sacrifice
No matter how expensive we'd still pay the price
The first word they say when we teach them to talk
The first steps they take when they've learned to walk
When we think back to the day they were born
They look so grown up in their school uniform
In their teens we teach them all the right ways
For they'll always remember their youthful days
We'll do just about anything to keep them amused
Try to explain the best way, when they get confused
When they're hungry we make sure they're fed
If they're tired we'll tuck them up safely in bed
When they're cold we'll make sure they get warm
By hugging them so they don't feel forlorn
When they hurt we'll take away the pain
For their comfort and feelings are the main
They depend on us to show and guide the way
They listen to and comment on what we have to say
Our opinions and views are sometimes pushed upon them
Believing this will make them better women or men
The love we'll both share will never perish
A relationship we'll always cherish
If we give it our all it will be a real pleasure
These precious years we must all treasure.

Sharon Caradice

MAMA

Oh! Mama tell me please
As you lay me down to sleep
Where does the sun go
Beyond the sea so deep
Then stars come out to light
The sky at night
Then when I awake
I may go and play
In the warmth of the sun
Before it sinks away.

Frank Shears

...LITTLE ANGELS...FOR CHARLOTTE

For all the cherished hearts, and little precious soulights . . .
they connect us in love.
All the innocent and loving little children . . .
each special little girl,
whose growing heart is far more precious than a diamond
and more lovely than a pearl . . .
and each special wild and mischievous
fun-loving little boy,
whose laughter brings joy . . .
playful at games and with toys,
all our girls and boys . . .
From babies gentle and happy, so awake,
aware, to new and magical a world, such as this . . .
With big eyes full of wonder,
at teddy bears and bright colourful flowers,
or the singing sweet sound of a mother's
lullaby, in dreamy hours . . .
Children are happy miracles, who bring and give
so much love,
with their awe at such simple wonders, like
feathers and wind chimes,
or fairy and magic animal stories,
and lovely silly little rhymes . . .
So beautiful are children, so many smiles.
Their future's ahead, like so many, many big miles . . .
Each sacred face, their expressions of joy and love,
a light within us.
Little earth angels, children's soulight in our hearts,
and illuminate us, each one a special bright spark . . .

Paul Holland

ONCE ...

The world was all pink, lit by a glowing fire
and an assuring nursery light.
All was warmth made deliciously soothing
by the scent of camphor that invited
sleep and calmed her feverish aching head.
She lay deep down, all wrapped in blankets
in the safe hiding place that was her bed
and listened as the sound of two soft sets
of footsteps came up the stairs. Anxious
Mummy and Daddy. She felt the tickle
of the blankets as Mummy tucked her in,
then heard Daddy say, 'She looks so little.'

> Once ... when we were very young,
> And I ask, 'Are we ever loved like
> this again?'

Margaret Hibbert

GOING OUT

We're going to have a day out,
Car's ready on the drive,
Two children put their shoes on
And through the doorway dive.

The big one runs straight to the car
And climbs into his seat,
The small one runs around the car
And sets off up the street!

At last we catch the little one
And pop her in the car,
Then search for keys, without which we
Would not get very far!

A third child strolls out of the door
And joins the other two,
Then number one decides that he
Must go back to the loo!

The boot's packed full of coats, clean clothes
(In case they should be sick),
We've books and sweets to keep them quiet . . .
That should do the trick.

With money, maps and mayhem,
There's nothing left to pack,
So let's be off, for soon it will be
Time to be heading back.

Catherine Champion

CHILDREN

The river flows, the tide is full,
the birds nest in the spring.
The flowers bloom, the apples hang,
the pulse of time goes on.

And on the hill the babe is born,
obeying Nature's call.
All living creatures must create,
a law cut into stone.

So the children come to us
but Man is unaware they must.
Logic's magic myth suggests
there is choice - there's not.

But having come they bless our lives,
they make our world complete
and now, perhaps, we have a choice
to nurture or to not.

If we do we learn to be,
to feel the flow of life.
They give us joy, they give us light
and pain and stress and hurt.

We must take care to let them be
not fit them in a mold
constructed by our wish
but let them grow without demand.

Let them take from us
the things they choose to take
and give them all we can.
Let them learn by what we are
not by what we say.

And then the moment comes,
they stand alone and love us
- hopefully.
In a moment time has passed,
no longer on our knee.
What joy to be themselves at last
in our hearts but free!

Jack W Oliver

GOLDEN YEARS

When I first became a granddad
I felt so very very old,
And friends and folk about me
Said I went quite grey and cold.
Now fifteen years have passed by
And those initial fears and dread,
Have by my six grandchildren
Stood my foolish notions on their head.
Exploring books by Roald Dahl
The doings of Postman Pat,
I have been introduced to Westlife
To Bono and Take That.
Whilst through the fields we've wandered
Watching countless sheep in flocks,
And picnicked in the meadows
Telling time by dandy clocks.
Together we've done homework
As I have put my brains in action,
Trying to explain the different
Whims to decimals and fractions
And then you have used your special skills
Bringing calm to my disorder,
As you confidently programme
My video recorder.
Through the days of fun and laughter
Days where tears have played a part,
Yes I thank all my six grandchildren
For keeping me, young at heart.

David A Garside

DAUGHTER DEAR

In this world, I have an angel
A perfect loving soul
With fire and strength
Though sensitive, with a tender heart

A treasure beyond compare
She has a restless spirit
Not unlike my own
She captivates me with her smile

When she's sad, it
Breaks my heart.
I want to have her near
I've missed so many chances

To tell her how I feel
The mistakes I made were many.
Sitting here I recall, them all.
We really belonged together.

The two of us
We both know that is true
We have waited for so long
One day it will all come right

In our hearts and minds we are close
That is crystal clear
For you my darling daughter
In this world, are the one I hold most dear.

Jeanette Jackson

OUR SON

Today is ours, but only today,
The gold at the end of the rainbow
Is always further on.
Our treasure is our son.
But the quick kiss on the cheek,
The game of hide and seek,
The sly little grin
When caught late creeping in
Are now treasured memories of the past.

For time takes its toll,
And he has now moved on to another world.
But the love we gave him
Oiled the wheels of life,
And most of his burdens
Will become less burdensome,
And with our love lose their weight.

Richard Forrest

THE CYCLE OF LIFE

Babies, so helpless and dependent upon us.
Their cute, angelic faces bring bundles of joy.
They cry when hungry, tired and in pain,
but giggle and smile when content with toys.

Quickly, they will grow to be children
before our very own eyes.
We teach them to read and write,
speak the truth and tell no lies.

As they become teenagers, times come under strain,
so we give them advice and guidance,
hoping they will make the right choices
and not leave everything to chance.

With the passage of time, they mature into adults,
able to stand on their own two feet.
Life beckons now to career, love and marriage.
When they become parents will see the cycle repeat.

Shabnam Yasmin (Baz)

CHILDREN

Most parents have no trouble having children,
Maybe a girl or a boy.
They are proud and filled with joy.
They are taught what is good and bad.
Some hope they will turn out like Dad.

But that doesn't mean they will be good.
Some make friends and are led astray.
Others make friends carefully and are okay.
Activities they do have a part to play.

Teaching them respect is another job parents do.
Also to be kind and polite too.
It's not really enough parents how they turn out,
Though when it comes,
They cause such shame leaving parents in doubt.

Pamela Earl

THE BABY

A copy of mothers and fathers reflection
A perfect example of all in perfection
A baby so new in the world like an ocean,
Demanding nothing at all but devotion.
With eyes that are bright and mind that is strong,
It clings with a force that says I belong.

A perfect pure being unwrapped like a gift,
The miracle of life like a veil it will lift.
A pity one says that its innocence won't last,
The future creeps up and the dreams in the past
The world will corrupt and the vision will fade,
The child is an adult through sin it must wade.
But the stronger the heart and determined the mind
The heart of a newborn the man will then find.

Sonia Sacre

LOVEABLE ROGUE

Joshua is my youngest boy
A rogue in all his glory
To list his devilish attributes
I would need to write a story

He's handsome and very loveable
Very cheeky in his own way
He makes friends very easily
And his moods change with the day

Many a tantrum he will throw
On the PlayStation he goes to town
His temper gets the better of him
He bangs controls and throws them down

His patience isn't very good
But he's only nine years old
Teach and tell him with respect
And he's willing to be told

He's a torment with his sister Emma
And he irritates Liam his brother
No one escapes his tormenting
Not even myself or his mother

But he's not the worst kid in the world
He's quite jolly and just loves fun
My love is unconditional for life
Simply because, he's Joshua - my son!

M B Powell

HUNTINGTOWER FIELDS, ALMONDBANK
(For Geraldine)

In time to come, when we are gone
In this same field of summer song
Where we once laughed and children ran,
Your child will be a woman
And my child will be a man.

The horse, no longer, will have wings
Shining, silver, in the sun,
The babbling stream, no danger, now
Where once a child would run.
And looking back, will you smile
As if by this you will keep
The memory of a lover's kiss
And of dreaming without sleep.

Shall we meet there again, I know not
Though, in time to come
And when we are gone
In this same field of summer song
Where we once laughed and children ran,
Your child will be a woman
And my child will be a man.

Scott Martin

GOD BLESS THE CHILDREN

I see the baby in the pram
And it makes me say
Who am I?
I once was a baby like you
With black curly hair
And eyes of blue
But look at me now
I'm fat like a ball
And my hair is like snow.
So I look at my watch
It is ten to three
I've got to go home
And make the tea
For my beautiful wife, called Margaret.

Kenneth Mood

TINY HANDS

Happiness comes in many forms, and nearly all are free,
Watching children playing on the beach is happiness for me,
To see their smiling faces, and lovely golden tans,
When they come running to me, holding crabs in tiny hands.

Hearing excited voices, as rocky pools are searched for more
The squealing with excitement, as they run along the shore,
Watching spellbound faces, enthralled at Punch and Judy show,
Takes my memory racing back, to holidays long ago.

Summertime may leave us, but happiness never will
Because long and happy memories, our mind will always fill.

G W Bailey

HAPPY BIRTHDAY SARAH!

How wonderful at last to lean upon the threshold of fifteen
So innocently filled with joys, untainted by the evil boys!
How far away seem childhood dreams of Fairyland and silver streams -
Of Santa Claus in coat so red who left you presents by your bed.
It seemed the sun shone every day as fun and laughter came your way.

And now it's homework, theatre, friends, activity that never ends
Pop stars to meet, the world to roam, art to explore and, of course,
                                         the Dome.
Beauty to share on woodland hills - the trembling of golden daffodils.
Football to watch, TV to view - so little time, so much to do.
How wonderful at last to lean upon the threshold of fifteen!

Eileen M Pratt

OUR BABY

My eeny weeny darling, whatever makes you tick?
I look at you for hours, but can't quite get the trick,
Your birth is hid in mystery, a mini-world and all
Of this world's strange creation responds to your loud call.

Your tiny fingers wondrous, they grip so tight my own,
Have we produced this marvel, is that the seed we've sown?
Epitome of humanity, are you the cosmic child,
The herald of the future, a spirit free and wild?

I hear you coo in candour, enraptured by your smile
I leave the world behind me, these things can wait a while,
And gaze on fascinated at what life has in store,
I vow to love and serve you, now and forever more.

Your body's small perfection I hold with awe and fear,
Lest I unheeding, careless, bring on a pain or tear,
You miniature magnifico have stolen my heart away,
My life has changed completely, my night has turned to day.

Around your crib we hover, souls out of time and mind,
Surrounded by the angels that you have left behind
In the harmonious Heaven where all is bright and fair,
You hint at coming glories with dreams you brought from there.

Emmanuel Petrakis

THE LITTLE MADAM

Three years old and cute and she knows it
Using grown-ups for her own ends
Telling tales and getting Granddad into trouble
By reporting his swear words from the shed

Now remember to watch what you say
Her hearing is very acute
She will report what you said about a neighbour
In the local shop

The call just when there is
A good film on the television
There is a monster in my bed
And I am thirsty

Now there is a play school to be chosen
Our little girl is beginning to grow up
At meals now it's
Mrs Parsons says . . .

Hours spent sitting holding hands
By her bedside
This time it's measles
Then that nasty cough that goes on and one

Her first party dress
The lump in the throat as she
Acts in a nativity play
And prompts the others

We try to remember but soon
These times are gone
Thank goodness for old photographs
Was she ever as small as that?

John Of Croxley

THE JOY YOU BRING

The joy you bring is heart warming,
Your smile, your laugh, your cheekiness,
How anyone could not want you is unbelievable,
The glee in your eyes says is all,
Yes you have disabilities and people don't understand,
But just because you're different doesn't mean you should be shunned,
You give as much love if not even more,
You put warmth in our hearts and fill up our days
We will love you forever and always be there,
There's so much love that we all share.

Sandra Pickering

HERITAGE OF THE LORD 'CHILDREN'

Child so helpless
More precious than gold
Gift from God
To be washed, fed and clothed.
Little eyes, little feet
Pleading eyes for that special treat
Sometimes laughter, sometimes tears
Winning ways not knowing fears.
Responsibility to parents, mould child
As he grows, future destiny God alone knows.
Gracious and loving
Parents need to be strong
Child is your offspring, with pride you may see
Someone climbing high in society.
Yet again, although parents implore
May witness ability pushed
Out the door.
Prayer is the answer, never give in
Some day, some time that soul
You may win.

Children are a heritage of the Lord
Prodigal Son returned
To warm welcome
From a waiting father.
Don't give up on your children
Keep a beacon burning every day
You may see your wayward child returning.

Frances Gibson

GIGGLEBUG AND GRUMBLEWEED

Dancing with a strained grace
Lips drawn tightly
Painted lightly
Effort etching elfin face
Tightly holding hair assembled
Fonteyn, Pavlova, resembled?
In pumps beribboned
Little diamond
To the music keeping pace
Spangled net and satin bodice
Pink and pale, demeanour modest
Showing all these months have taught her
Lace and frill, indulgence bought her
Sensitive and lively daughter
I puzzle while I aim to lead
Gigglebug and Grumbleweed.

Norine Bleakley

AND BROKE MY HEART...

My little nine month wonder
came forth into my arms
and broke my heart with happiness
face tear-stained by his charms

And in his crib a'sleeping
his helpless frame unfolds
and broke my heart with fears for him
at what the future holds

His first steps took unsteady
his arms reach out for me
and broke my heart with fervent love
to catch his hands so wee

His schooldays came a'calling
the first bell gave a ring
and broke my heart with worry
of what each day would bring

And when he started working
with wage, to me he ran
and broke my heart with loving pride
my child was now a man

And soon engaged to marry
his bride to be was sweet
and broke my heart with joy and peace
that such a girl he'd meet

But fate designed too early
an illness for his death
and broke my heart with sorrow
as he took his final breath.

Cherry

LITTLE STAR

Come little child sit upon my knee
And before you go to bed to rest,
Look up into the sky,
Can you see the star that shines so high?
You wonder why it shines so bright,
It is to guide you little mite,
For you to look and to see,
Also to wonder where dear Jesus can be.

I M Lathan

ROUND AND ROUND THE GARDEN

Before we two knew,
You three were there,
   Mouths open to be fed,
   Minds longing to be read
   to every blooming night.
Yawl, bawl, crawl, scrawl,
Cats' tails to be pulled,
Nappies to be filled,
   Why this? Why that?
Why don't you ever sleep,
   More like!

Before we two knew,
You three were gone,
   Umbilical cord to shed,
   Something called 'street cred'
   to give you main and might.
Booze, cruise, woos, blues,
New heights to be scaled,
Oceans to be crossed,
   Try this, try that,
Try giving you advice?
   Fat chance!

Before we two knew,
You three were back,
   But now, as Wordsworth said,
   Child father of the man, instead
   to ease your parents' plight.
Spare, share, bear, care,
The pillows to be propped,
Shopping to be got,
   Now this, now that,
Now we can go in peace,
   Job done!

Peter Davies

THROUGH HER EYES

We walked and she chatted endlessly on the way
'Look a broken slab and that one's grey
Two are wobbly, I'll fall if I play.'
Then by the river path we went
And stopped and looked at the broken fence.

A snail and slug took her gaze
She chatted on quite unfazed.
'Why has one got a house on its back
Look, the other has left a slimy track.'
We fed the ducks, how they thronged
Shortly joined by the bullying swans.

She skipped and collected pretty stones
Two almost identical, nearly clones.
Each and every step produced some new-found treasure
A leaf, a flower, a log with earwig resting at leisure.

This little, pink-cheeked child blew my mind asunder
And gave me hours of perfect wonder
I had forgotten how to see
My observation returned by a child of three
Now my mind runs free filled with receptivity.

Gloria Hargreaves

SIX POUNDS TEN

My sweet baby, he's so small and helpless
He came into this world, naked and wealthless
I look at his tiny hands, and I can't believe
That by loving your daddy, you were conceived
Inside Mummy's womb, you divided and became
Arms and legs, beating heart, your own tiny brain
It's still a wonder to me, each passing day
That one small seed, could grow that way
It's all God's doing, yet it's hard to explain
All that mighty pushing, all that pain
But it's soon forgotten, as family members just stare
At that tiny helpless baby lying there
Perfect fingers, each perfectly formed nail
Searching into doctor's eyes, did anything fail.
'He's a healthy little boy, weighs six pound ten.'
Then a nurse enquires, 'Will you do this again?'
The pain's all forgotten, my limbs no longer lister,
'Oh yes, I shall my dear, he'll need a baby sister.'

Ann Hathaway

HAPPY BIRTHDAY

I'm counting the days to my birthday.
I've drawn a red ring round my date
On the calendar. I'm so excited!
Four days now and I shall be eight!

Mother will come and awake me
With greetings at seven o'clock.
I'll open some parcels at breakfast,
Then wait for the postman to knock.

I hope that the day will be sunny,
That nothing will hurt or annoy.
I want it to be an occasion
Which others can also enjoy.

I think it will be a great pity
To do any work on my day,
But, when it's all finished, I'll play hard,
And go to bed late if I may.

My best friends will come to my party.
We'll have fruit and custard for tea,
And an iced cake with candles. My birthdays
Come round far too slowly for me!

Dora Hawkins

THE WAITING ROOM

Here we sit
In the waiting room
Dishevelled
Disillusioned
With everything around

The sign
Pointing to the door
Says
'The old'

The sign
Pointing to the other door
Says
'The new'

Clearing of throats
Shufflings of feet
Embarrassed staring at the floor

No-one dares ask the other
'Quo vadis'?

Non dialogue leads to
Unconsciousness

And then
A child
   A boisterous
   Spontaneous
   Adventurous
Child
A Universal Child
Venturing to the toy box
Drags all the toys
Upon the floor
And playfully makes constructs
Not seen before

Of things old
In new configurations
Gradually
Surreptitiously
Apologetically
Even
All the rest
Take part
Calling up
In their playfulness
Undreamt of
Life-formations
Bound for the exits
To the new
In the waiting room
Of life
Between the ages.

John Crowe

SHEREEN'S FOOLING AROUND

Who is that girl running to school,
Who's just fallen onto the ground?
She was running too fast, as she was too late,
Because she'd been fooling around!
Who is that girl talking all day?
Did she invent the word, 'sound'?
At least we can hear wherever she is
And know where she's fooling around!
Who is that girl who fell in the lodge,
While chasing that big black hound,
And left her sneaker stuck in the mud?
While she was fooling around!
Who is that girl with the nice new watch,
Which kept time 'cos it need never be wound?
Until the day it was worn in the bath,
While she was fooling around!
Who is that girl with a piggy bank,
Who likes to save each 'penny pound'?
But thinks she can save whilst spending the lot,
While she is fooling around!
Who is that girl at the dancing school,
Learning each step with a leap and a bound
And occasionally going head over heals?
While she is fooling around!
Who is that girl working hard at school,
Learning so much she's getting profound?
It just proves how sensible she can be,
When she doesn't fool around!

Christopher Head

OUR FOUR

We have four children
Two girls and two boys
Over all the years
We've had lots of laughs
And lots of tears
We love them all dearly.

All too soon they go to school
Learn to read and write
Then they bring home girlfriends
Boyfriends, soon there's talk of
Weddings. Too soon, I thought.
Where will the money come from
We will find it somehow
What a sad day when it comes
Our eldest getting wed.
How proud to see how lovely
She looked on her daddy's arm.
Now after our forty-five years wed
Our children have all gone
Married now with children
Of their own.
Now we have so many
Grandchildren to see,
Bringing joy to all the family.

J M Drinkhill

FLIPPIN' KIDS

Years ago they gave us great joy,
Babies were born, a girl or boy
And everyone was happy.
Now, if their sex is not forecast,
Some parents would be quite downcast,
Yet, few need to wash a nappy.

In the past they grew up slowly
And learned more about things holy,
Tables and bead frames were in vogue.
No sooner now they are at school
Than calculators are the rule,
Computers used by any rogue.

Were children better long ago?
It's very difficult to know,
Their opportunities were few.
Or, are today's sometimes spoilt brats
Prepared to be the next 'fat cats'
Because, it's the 'cool' thing to do?

H P

JOHN THE SNOWMAN

Daniel 'n' Connor playing in the snow
Little faces, little cheeks all aglow!
Roly-poly, roly-poly - tumbling in the snow!
Then rolling giant snowball - fast as they can go!

So excited at building their own snowman
Boys don't hear music from ice-cream van!
Daniel adds a crooked carrot to make a funny nose!
Connor uses black buttons to mark out eyes and clothes!
Daniel's daddy's scarf to keep their snowman warm,
Wearing Connor's dad's chefs hat, snowman looks quite foreign!

They name him John, then both yawn, it's time for bed!
'Night night John! See you in the morn!' Chorused two sleepy heads.
Soon they'll be warm and cosy, lose their little red noses
And two little sets of frozen pink tootsie-toes!

Patricia Cairns Laird

OUR SCOTT

Sunday 30th April was a lovely
sunny morn,
An exciting day for daddy and I
'twas the day that you were born.
Nannan called you 'little speedy'
you couldn't wait to see the world,
the midwife said 'Bet you're disappointed
this baby's not a girl!'
How we couldn't wait to hold you
your daddy and I,
the moment that we cuddled you
you would no longer cry.
Daddy took you to the window,
so the world you'd see
a special quality you possessed
we knew our pride and joy you'd be.
We hadn't chose a name for you
for you took us by surprise,
a choice of three we couldn't decide
for our little baby blue eyes.
Soon your schooldays came around and
we had to learn to let go,
of our red-haired little darling
on to much successes he did go!
Remembering your first class in school
you'd bring a smile to your teacher's face
She'd often phone for us to collect you
saying 'I just can't keep him awake.'
For when she read a story off to sleep you'd go
whether sitting at a table or on the
carpet you know.
The years passed by then you were bullied
your trusted teachers let you down.
Your strength of character and determination
became admired by all around.

Those bad times are in the past now yet
you have proved once more.
The exceptional strength of character
of our son that we adore.
Wherever life may take you
at times when we're apart
our love will always go with you
forever in our hearts.
One wish that we have for you
is one day your dreams may all come true.
Just as ours did one April morn,
when God chose us the day you were born.

We love you more than life itself -
our precious son - Scotty.

Michele Simone Fudge

THE GIFT OF MY CHILDREN FROM GOD

From birth I loved, watched and touched
I remember lots of memories
That's deep inside my heart
To know that I'm your mother
Was a privilege from the start.

I've been your nurse, teacher and guide,
And I've laughed with you all and cried.
I found your first teeth
And, put a coin under your pillow when you were fast asleep
I helped you to say your first words 'mama' and 'dada'
And, was with you as you took your first steps from the settee.

You splashed so much in the bath
You soaked the carpet and my clothes
But, to know how much joy it gave
I laughed and laughed too.

We would lie in front of the fire at night
With your crayoning books and pencils and all the jigsaws out
We would stay until it was time for bed
And then we would say our prayers
Say goodnight, God bless, and turn out the light.

When you became teenagers it was hard for me and you
But, in the hope of what I tried to teach you
Your independence has grown.

When I look at you now, I still love you all
From the day you were born just as you are.
You're getting on with your lives now you have left home
And to see what you've come through
I'm so glad I'm your mother,
Of my son and two daughters,
And I've just been there for you with God too.

J Carter

LITTLE GUY

Saturday night
I am dancing with
Delight.
With guess who?
My darling,
One and a half year old
Nephew.

Bernadette O'Reilly

LITTLE CHILDREN

Little children, what a joy
Like glorious flowers in a field
God gifted them for you to love
And tell them of His protective shield.

They know nothing of the apple
That Eve took from the tree
But as they grow they will know
Good and evil like you and me.

If we can forget what we know
And let the children show the way
Their innocence will do the rest
Then we will have heaven on earth one day.

The asp and Eve destroyed true life
And the spell of knowledge did the rest
Temptation is the spell to break
A child's true love will do the rest.

A F Mace

KIDS

When we were kids we made mud pies,
Found plenty of things to do with our lives,
Built a house or den, out of fallen trees,
So young and innocent, so easy to please.
Out of rose petals we'd make disgusting scent,
We thought it great, all over us it went.
Food in the den was laid on the floor,
There were blackberries, groundnuts and lots more.
To play in we had shoes, with one or two holes,
When walking along stones would go up the soles.
We'd go for a picnic, nothing posh,
A few jam sandwiches, a drink of squash.
About six mam would shout, 'Time to come in',
We'd plead to stay, but knew we wouldn't win.
In the bath we were scrubbed, got very clean,
As you can guess we weren't very keen.
Supper then bed, mam never heard a peep,
Had such a busy day, we fell fast asleep.

J P Williams

STORM PHOTOGRAPHS
(For my niece, Storm Elizabeth Pearson)

Oh, sweet child. How innocent you are, lying in your brother's arms.
So unaware of your future, the dreams that will become you.
The future lies only in your waking, and the love that lies around
you in the faces of your brothers and sister, of your parents.
You are so young, not long walking, not long before you learn to
run with the breeze to fly kites high in the sky.
Not long now before words change from Lala and Po to those
learnt at school and from library books.
There is no greater thing than the knowledge learnt from one day
to the next, the knowledge to live in happiness.
And, my dearest child, you will not walk onto life's path without
many a loving hand to help guide you.
For all of life, you will know triumphs and disappointments, but
there will be many who will congratulate and comfort you.
But now, gentle Storm, you sleep peacefully in your elder brother's
arms, with your night-time sucky thing giving you extra comfort,
and wrapped up in pink fleece to keep you warm against the
winter's chill, making you bright in the greying light.
Sleep on, young one, sleep on until the sun comes to greet you
with warmth, and a loving hug from your mother's arms.

Angela G Pearson

DREAMER

On my report card
In primary two
They said I was a dreamer
I wasn't sure
If this was good or bad
But now
As I picture my parents
As they read the card
Sitting in the garden
Next to the honeysuckle
And the initial look
Of parental concern
Before smiling at each other
I think
It was a good report card that year.

Tracy Patrick

ALWAYS AND FOREVER MINE

As I held you
My tiny little bundle of elation
Made up of five fingers, five toes
And two very loving parents.
I was bewildered, so marvelled
By your pure beauty
And though we were strangers
Brought together by a miracle of life.
I was in love with you
Overcome by protection
So much so
That my dilated eyes
Formed an eternal seal to your tiny body
And however big you would grow
God himself wouldn't break it.
I was so in love with you
You made me feel like nothing I'd felt before
And my life would never be the same
That still hasn't altered
But I wouldn't have it any other way.

Charlotte Western-Reed

JONATHAN AND DANIEL, THE LIGHT OF MY LIFE

Jonathan and Daniel,
The light of my life.
The fruit of my loins,
The seed of my seed,
Flesh of my flesh,
And most of all, they're mine.

Mine all mine, that no one else can take,
They are my sons, of course!
What else can I say.
I love them this much,
God loves them this much,
Their openness, honesty and enthusiasm,
Has taught me a lot.

I thank God each day for these boys of mine,
These boys who are the light of my life,
The fruit of my loins,
The seed of my seed,
Flesh of my flesh,
And most of all, they're mine.

Mine that no one can take,
Mine throughout eternity.
No one can part us, and depart us,
As this bond of ours,
Is as strong as a beat,
I love them this much,
God loves them this much,
I thank God each day for these boys of mine,
These boys who are the light of my life,
And most of all, they're mine,
Mine all mine.

Evelyn Ringrow

TODAY'S CHILD

Small little people
With very large voice
Youthful joviality
Thoughts contrite
Putting adults in place
As unquestionability
They smilingly rejoice
Without worry or fear
Hesitance not a trace

Today's child bubbles
Life is embraced
Long gone restraints
Imposed by elders
To bygone times
Long displaced
Till energetic exhaustion
Pours always over
Causing total distaste.

Gary J Finlay

THREE CAMEOS
(Dedicated to my children)

He sighed and stretched, there's work to be done
He said to himself. In the garden, he found,
As good as gold, his five-year old son
Absorbed in brushing their patient hound.
Unseen, he watched him, in the sun,
Then Ben came racing across the ground
Knowing he'd have the greatest fun
Being lifted, hugged and swung around.

And their joyous laughter filled the air.

She was only three and shy. She stood quite still
As her father went forward to meet his guests.
Her mother turned, held out her hand. 'Come, Jill,'
She said gently, 'Come and don't be afraid.'
Then felt a tiny hand steal into hers.
They went forward together and a bond was made.

And trust is a joy that two must share.

Birthday cake cut and presents galore,
Ribbons and wrappings all over the floor
But now it was time for uncle to go
And how to thank him she did not know
But suddenly, waiting at the door,
A daisy, at her feet, she saw.
She picked it quickly and ran to his side,
Full of excitement. 'For you!' she cried
And raced away to wave once more.
And now, she thought, I'm really four!

And these three joys are beyond compare.

J M Craufurd-Stuart

A Child's Gift

The first smile from a child
is one to remember,
'twill be in your mind all your days,
you'll never forget
be it June or November
the first words that they manage to say.

Their bubbling smile,
the light from their eyes
the grip from their tiny clenched fist,
these can all turn us on
and bring forth the sighs
like the time we were first held and kissed.

But these blossoming days
don't last very long
and quite soon they are crawling and walking,
they steadily grow
and soon are quite strong
and before you're aware, they are talking.

It is then off to school
in their new uniform
and friends, in their class, they will make,
that's the parents' sad time
when they have to conform
and the hold, on their kids, they must shake.

And grown up they now are
in such a short time
it is then that their parents feel old,
their kids are now grown
and through life they'll be fine,
yet the tie with their parents they'll hold.

Leslie Holgate

A LIFETIME OF LOVE

There can be no other experience,
Like seeing a baby born.
You don't know whether to laugh or cry,
Your heart feels as though it is torn.

In the first few months of their lives,
We are full of worry and fret.
Why is the baby crying now?
Is it earache or a tummy upset?

We must cherish these moments we have with them,
Because these moments do not last.
They no sooner take their first step in life,
Then they grow up oh so fast.

We teach them how to walk and talk,
We teach them wrongs from rights.
We teach them how to dress themselves,
And show them wonderful sights.

They are made from the love of two people,
And they give their love in return.
You give them love throughout their lives,
But sometimes you have to be firm.

We can only advise our children,
To save them toil and strife,
And no matter what mistakes they make,
They have our love for the whole of their life.

R Beaman

THE CHILDREN ARE OUR FUTURE

The children are our future
We must teach them right
From the first thing in the morning
Till the last thing at night

The children are our future
We must teach them right from wrong
Teach them how to live in peace
And we know they can't go wrong

The children are our future
Sent down from heaven up above
To fill our lives with happiness
To fill our hearts with love.

Greeny 2001

THE PLEASURE OF A BABY

There are not many pleasures
That one can compare
To the loving of a baby
And simply being there

From birth to early nursing
Where every need is met
Though sometimes quietly cursing
It's as good as it can get

To see a baby growing
The pride when it can walk
The joy of love that binds you
The thrill when it can talk

And then the little person
Like a butterfly appears
The product of a parents' love
To fly despite the fears

You'll never cease to worry
When a baby's fully grown
You'll never cease to have the joy
That in its birth you've known.

Ray Ryan

BABY SITTING

I'm very fond of tiny tots,
Little blue-eyed ones - like little forget-me-knots.
I nurse them and cuddle them up tight,
But my baby sitting is over
When mums and dads come home at nights.
Little ones need so much love
'Mr Teddy Bear they seem to like a lot,
And Barbie Dolls are not forgot.
Some little tinkers laugh - then scream,
I keep my cool in all their bouts,
Well tots are good at trying us sitters out.
Some want to see TV till late,
But Mum said have them in bed at eight.
So I get out a story book
I sit on their beds and read
'Goldilocks and the Three Bears' many like,
They soon then go off to sleep
And I turn out the lights.
Time then for me to have a little peace
But no, that's not to be,
For often down the stairs they come
Saying 'I want a glass of water please.'

Marion Staddon

YOUR BABY

Your baby is a precious soul
Who sweetly comes along
To wind herself around your heart
And teach you right from wrong
She captures everything that's you
And will not let you go
Because, though weak, her strength is much
The strongest that you know
Her little arms, her little legs
The magic of her charms
The very soft warm feel of her
As she nestles in your arms
On through life with her you go
As parents by her side
Until she finds she does not need
You there to be her guide
So then you have to fondly take
A backward step and be
The person that's at home for her
And gently set her free.

Royston E Herbert

JUST THREE

Life isn't easy when you're growing up and three,
there are places you want to go, places where really
and truly, I just shouldn't be!
Mum gets cross and angry, she hasn't now got so
much time for me, because very often,
someone else is sitting on her knee.

And there's another thing, they think I'm big and grown,
but I do like to snuggle close, and have her for my own;
don't get me wrong, I love the baby, she's really small
and cute, but when I poke her and wake her up,
then I'm really up the chute!

I'm not big enough for school yet, and though
playgroup is fun, they jump up and shut the doors
where I really want to run; I have to share
all the time, toys, slides, bikes and things,
have they forgotten that I'm only three,
and always, always have to win?

Still, it really is alright between my mum and me,
for I know she 'specially loves me, when she lifts me
on her knee; when she hugs me close and runs
her fingers through my hair, because although I'm
bad at times, I know she's really glad I'm there!

Catherine Riley

FRANK

Frank is such a bubbly child, he'd stop you feeling blue,
The questions that he asks, would put you all askew,
Innocence exudes from every word he speaks,
He wants an answer to his quest, immediate he seeks,
What does the world look like from Frank's eluding eyes?
Dreaming off down through the woods, catch winging butterflies,
Why aren't they all just like Frank, an endearing little chap,
Never ever clip his wings, his heart would surely snap.

W Curran

NEW LOVE AT MY AGE? NEVER!

I never thought I'd see the day
I'd know the Tweenies each by name,
Or down the pub I would betray
I'd got a Bob the Builder game.

Ousted from my 'lair' - my private grief!
The decorators ran amok:
My bookshelves gone! New leitmotif
Of themed Jemima Puddleduck.

I've breadth of knowledge recondite
Of all the makes and styles of buggies,
And where to find the shops that might
Have offers on the price of Huggies!

From early dawn I creep, half-slept,
To spend my day in baby talk,
Read 'Ladybirds' I've so long kept -
I've twice re-read my 'Doctor Spock'.

The nappy change, the colic fraught, her
Projectile sick - don't count the cost:
I can't begrudge my own granddaughter,
For time with her is never lost.

Maybe I've gone a bit senile:
In silence, watching her mobile,
Besotted, by her cot awhile
I wait upon her day's first smile . . .

Patrick Brady

THE BEST AGE

I have always believed eighteen months to be the best age,
This is the time before children have reached the tantrum stage.
Probably walking, using signs, while saying their first words,
Doing everything possible to make themselves heard.

Childish innocence goes as adult attributes acquired,
Entering teenage phase, with lots of habits undesired.
Through it all unconditional love to offspring given,
Young develop, follow the pre-planned journey of living.

S Mullinger

THE JOY OF CHILDREN

Months have gone by
Weeks have gone by
For me waiting for the
Summer holiday
Soon it will be
Time for pleasure
Time for joy
Time for happiness
And time to enjoy other
Relatives conversation
Conversing of the old times
And
Conversing about the new times
But all I am waiting for
Is my summer holiday.

Fahad Eqbal

LIFE'S EXCHANGE

A child's shy chuckle
Adult hearts melt tenderly
Renewal through love.

Brenda Dove

THE JOY OF CHILDREN

Dimpled fingers, wrinkled nose,
Silk-soft ringlets, curled up toes,
When your child is born - to love and care
'Tis a miracle beyond compare.

Tottering toddler, learning fast
In a world of wonder, oh so vast,
Tumbles, tantrums, giggling glee
Fun and laughter, what a spree.

Schooldays come, knowledge grows:
What holds the future no one knows.
The joy of youth, the pain of love
Needs precious handling with kid glove.

Your arms they ache when they are small
Your heart near breaks if they should fall
In times of trouble or of grief
Your love still enfolds beyond belief.

Poignant problems and cares incense
Life has its moments so intense
You are there to care and share
When your child is finding life unfair.

A bond unbroken all through life
The joy of a child - in spite of strife,
Cannot be broken come what may
A chord so strong outshines the day.

Comes the time when your *child* gives birth
A new cycle starts of joy and mirth
Such happiness it never ceases
For the joy of children just increases!

Mollie D Earl

GROWTH

When I was a child - unable
then to act like a child
expected to be a parent
now adult - can act wild.

Robert D Shooter

LEAP! BEFORE I DISAPPEAR

One very windy afternoon
A cat was playing with a balloon
Quite suddenly the wind blew whoosh!
The balloon and cat rose with a swoosh!
His friend the frog jumped on his back,
'Please take me too,' he said, piggy-back!

Soaring together airborne in the sky,
Wafting, weaving, way up high,
A colourful pair green frog, red cat,
Whizzing around like trapeze acrobats,
Round, up and down then round yet again,
I wish I could fly home, thought the frog, like a wren,
He felt sick, tapped the cat on the back, rat-a-tat,
'I want to go back, but not to land squashed flat with a splat!'

They saw Mr Rainbow, 'Please help us get down!'
'Sit upon me,' he said 'until I touch down!'
'After a shower I sometimes appear
For you I'll come out to take you from here.'
Slowly he drifted across the sky,
A far-reaching arc for all to espy,
Vivid, brilliant hue almost to the ground,
Then hovered a while over children's playground,
'Hurry lads!' he boomed. 'Leap, before I disappear
Fading away into the atmosphere.
Remember, be bold let go of something you hold,
Than regret it after an accident, tenfold.
That also applies to anything that rolls into road,
Better to lose it than lie hurt under truck load!'
Thank you Mr Rainbow,' chorused green frog and red cat,
'You are wise! We were silly not to think of that!'

Hilary Jill Robson

HOME FOR TEA

Peter Pugh was a pirate bold,
As fearless as could be,
He sailed the mighty Spanish Main
But went home in time for tea.

He climbed to the top of the tallest mast
No matter how rough the sea,
But he always made sure he was down again
In time to go home for tea.

In the pirate ship, The Saucy Sal,
He made his enemies flee,
And no matter how fierce the battle was
He always went home for tea.

With the Jolly Roger hoisted high
He set sail for Dundee
To seize ten barrels of marmalade
But he still came home for tea.

Peter Pugh was a pirate bold
And his mother would agree,
And even on days when he sailed round the world
He had to come home for tea.

Sheila Bryant

THE DRAGON

The dragon looks a fearful chap
But he really isn't bad,
In fact now I come to think of it
He really looks quite sad.

He puffs and pants and snorts a bit
And makes a dreadful noise,
It really is alarming for little girls and boys,
But when you look at him
Through all those clouds of smoke
With his great big feet and long green tail
He really is a joke.

So if you see a dragon,
Don't think of him as bad,
He may be making all that noise
Just because he's sad.

Phillip Storey

FROGGY CHORUS

Come on chaps,
Squash together,
Move along,
Let's get croaking,
And begin a song.

Is everybody ready?
Keep in tune,
Keep in time,
Bill please sit still,
You're breaking up the line.

Let's warm up then,
Croak an 'A' for me,
Bob, don't catch that fly,
You've already eaten tea.

That was a very good performance,
But it's just such a shame,
Since we lost our best soloist,
We are just not the same.

What was that maiden thinking,
To go and kiss our Vince?
She just about destroyed our choir,
Turning the lead into a prince!

Kay Challenor

MILLICENT PUMPKIN SNITCH

Young Millicent Pumpkin Snitch,
offspring of a wizened old witch.
Would often borrow Mum's broom,
whoosh, and off she would zoom.

Scouring strange scary lands,
taking frightened children's hands.
Leading them off, to distant caves,
where, to their immense surprise,
they would dance all night long,
with kings, queens and knaves.

Partying at the royal ball for frightened kids,
when, after a night of mischievousness,
fairy dust would settle, on sleepy eyelids.
And children, waking to reality again,
knew their lives would never be the same.
After being visited by Millicent Pumpkin Snitch,
A young, white witch, with a most peculiar name.

Danny Coleman

MUMS AND BABIES

Sammy, baby harp seal,
Three months old and fluffy white
He slipped, slithered down the frozen ice,
To see his mum Judy hunting for fish,
She popped up and she gave Sammy
A loving kiss. They live in Canada's frozen gulf.

Meg, Martha, Mary are three sisters,
Loving lion cubs, a mother's pride,
Mum looks and smells, cuddle close
To her lion cubs she suckles each one,
Meg is very proud of her lion cubs
Mum pounces on her prey, attacks giraffe or rhino.

Baby bear cub twins were born
Hairless and blind, small as a rat
With black noses, Holly and Honey
Two white polar bears, and there's mother Amy
As she holds them safe in her giant paws.

Christine Shurey

NIL

'Have a go on my computer,' my grandson said,
'Just press that little button, keep pressing
Until he's dead.'
Well, I pressed and pressed that button,
Heard a funny noise, 'Bing, Bong'.
'No, no,' said my grandson, 'you're doing it all wrong.'
'First move it to the left, now over to the right,
Quick press now Gran, you've got him in your sight.'
'But darling, he keeps moving, he just will not keep still.'
That's it the game is over, my final score
Is nil.

J P Williams

A RHYME FOR A KITTEN

Little one, pretty one, where have you been?
Little one, pretty one, what have you seen?
'Down through the garden and over the fence,
Out in the meadow where daisies are dense.'

Little one, pretty one, what did you find?
'Only some feathers a bird left behind.'
Little one, pretty one, what have you heard?
'Little lambs bleating and song of a bird.'

Little one, pretty one, where did you look?
'Meadow and hedgerow and down by the brook.
I hunted all morning until I was tired,
But never a glimpse of the things I desired.'

'No river, no palace, no queen have I seen
But surely a kitten may look at a queen?
Next time I'll be lucky, she may come my way.'
Little one, pretty one, come home and play!

Kathleen M Hatton

THE GNOME

I'm a garden gnome, who sits alone
On a rock in the middle of a pond.
I was found in a box, broken to bits
But now repaired every piece fits.
I bask in the sun and watch the fish swim
And little frogs jump with elevated spring.
I've a scarlet hat, trousers blue,
I was second-hand, but now I'm like new.
When summer ends and north winds blow
I'm put in the shed, away from the snow
My colours may fade, but a quick lick of paint
I'll be ready and waiting
Life's just great.

Glennis Stokes

HEAVENS ABOVE

When at night
I'm tucked in tight
My parents give me a hug
And I feel snug
I suddenly cast my eye
To the vast sky
So many magical stars
I wonder which is Mars?
The stars twinkling so bright
My heart feeling light.

And I want to up there fly
I don't know why
But it would be fascinating
As well as exciting!
The stars shining brighter than ever
It was now or never
It suddenly seemed a very dark night
And I felt I was *in flight*
As in bed I lay
I was whisked away.

Travelling through the *air*
With ease and not a care!
Suddenly - I felt doomed
When a loud voice - *boomed*
Are you alright *Jamie*!
I *shivered* - the stars speaking to me?
I looked *carefully* around
There was no other sound
But - *No* - it was my *dear old dad*
I had fallen *out of bed*!

Josephine Foreman

CANDLE NIGHT

Candle light
Candle night
Feet pass
To midnight mass
Bells ring
Choirs sing
A shepherd peeps
A baby sleeps
Children bring
Their love to Him
Emmanuel
Emmanuel
In the skies
Angels' eyes
Star light
Star night.

Breda Sullivan

JANET'S DOLL

You sit there in the chair
And sometimes on the floor
Always looking happy
Just like the day before.

You always have a smile
Your face is never sad
Even if you're dirty
And your hair is tied with rag.

Your dress it can be grubby
And your shoes may have no shine
But you don't seem to worry
Cos you're smiling all the time.

I love you in so many ways
That no one else can see
Because you're always happy
And you listen close to me.

So I will try to remember
Not to leave you on the floor
I will put you in the dolls' house
Before I close the door.

Diana Slater

BUTTERFLY

I see you there
So straight and tall
Looking just like
The belle of the ball

Long velvet dress
Of midnight blue
Beautiful girl
Is it really you?

Sparkling smile
And curls piled high
Such lovely grace
Brings tears to my eyes

Bouquet of gorgeous
Delicate hues
Matching your eyes
In shades of blue

Silver earrings
A necklace so fine
Is this butterfly
That daughter of mine?

This charming vision
Must be wrong
Where has my sweet
Funny tomboy gone?

She'll return tomorrow
No need to fear
She's only a bridesmaid
One day of the year!

Carolyn Fittall

MR LITTERBUG

I'm writing just to tell you
All about a nasty man
Who likes to spoil a country view
In every way he can:
They call him Mr Litterbug
Because he likes to roam
And leave behind the litter
He should have taken home!

If you wander in the countryside,
You'll see just what I mean
Old bottles and a plastic tide
Of litter where he's been:
He'll dump his soggy fish and chips
Bald tyre and rusty tin
Because he's not a man who tips
His litter in the bin!

He loves his country capers,
Enjoying Nature's treats;
And dropping all the papers
That wrapped his sticky sweets!
He'll leave behind his can of Coke
To clatter down the lane,
Because he's just a thoughtless bloke
With litter for a brain!

Nicholas Winn

NEIGHBOURS

Nod-dog lives at number 24,
Persian Chat-cat lives next door.
Every morning Nod-dog walks
round the park with Mrs Brown.
In Chat-cat's home Miss Mallow talks
saying 'I'll just pop into town.'
She takes her keys and locks the door;
Chat-cat sits smiling on the floor,
then swings the cat-door flap.
'I'm free. First a walk and then a nap.'
But Nod-dog wakes her, barking loud,
'I've had my walk! I'm strong! I'm proud!'
Chat-cat lifts a sleepy paw
and yawns, 'That noisy dog next door!'

Ruth Partington

In Celebration

Through a jungle of emotions
to a place a long, long way,
your sweet, loving devotion
carried children from dismay.

Although your heart wounded deeply,
you did strive to weave a home
'midst magic hills, which steeply
embraced green where we could roam.

Ever there and ever caring,
you bonded with compassion
the family by sharing
a strength far beyond ration.

How you managed, I do not know -
like you there is no other!
Enough to say that we owe
our lives to you, Dear Mother!

Perry McDaid

WE WENT SAILING

One day while I was playing in my bedroom, by myself,
I climbed upon my bed and took my teddies from the shelf,
I dressed them up like sailors, in uniforms of blue,
Then I lined them up and said 'I know what we can do,
We'll make my bed into a ship and we will sail the seas,'
So off we went, around the world, my faithful crew and me.
We went to many foreign lands and fought with pirates bold,
We even took some prisoners and locked them in the hold,
We went to Australia and caught a kangaroo,
Bought it back to London and put it in the zoo.
In Africa, the warriors attacked us from the beach,
So we hoisted up our sails and sailed right out of reach,
Then a whale attacked our ship and turned it upside down,
Good job that I've learnt to swim or else I might have drowned.
The best adventure of them all, was in the south of France,
We fought the French and Spanish too; they didn't stand a chance,
We sank their ships and took their gold, then gave it to the Queen,
She said we were the bravest crew that she had ever seen.
When the journey ended, for teddy bears and me,
I put them all back on the shelf and went downstairs for tea.

Jim Sargant

THE CROCODILE AND THE DENTIST

Did you ever see a crocodile
That shook with fear?
If you promise not to tell
I will whisper in your ear.
'He was afraid of the Dentist
can you believe that?'
He sat in the chair
and trembled like a cat who had just seen a mouse.

Did you ever see a crocodile
whose teeth did chat
when he opened up his mouth
he wished he was a mat that the cat sat on.

Did you ever see a Dentist
who shook with fear?
Well, I'll tell you now
with a crocodile so near
his hands did shake and his knees went queer.

So the crocodile and the dentist
shook with fear
they trembled like jelly and then ran like deer
for the door.

Joy Grant

Your Own Special Room

It's your own special room
Where you can say goodnight to the moon.
We've made it real special and so true
Just for a perfect angel, that's you.
The stars will guide you through the night
Making sure you'll be alright.
There are teddies galore
To keep you safe and secure.
If you get frightened it'll be OK
Mummy is only a dream away
Close your eyes and think of me
And
I'll be right by your side, you'll see.

Michelle Barnes

GEMIMA

Gemima was more than a treasure
We fetched her one day
In the spring
When farmer Brown's cat
Had her kittens
We chose her
Just the sweetest wee thing
We took her home
Mum said, 'You name her.'
Gemima I thought suits her fine
I loved her the moment I saw her
And as she grew we had such fun
She sleeps at the foot of my bed
Every night
And she wakes me
Each day morning comes
I give her a hug
And I whisper
'Gemima, you're my number one.'

Jeanette Gaffney

Run - Run

No 1   Have some fun - run, run
2 and 3 Skip to that tree
No 4   Now hop some more
5 and 6 Jump over the sticks
7 and 8 Climb over the gate
No 9   Stand in line
Now it's ten - we begin again!

Christine McBain

ANNA'S ROCKING HORSE SONG

Pony, pony, off we go
Pony, pony, don't go slow
Pony, it's a lovely day
Pony, pony, let us ride away.

Pony, pony, don't you stop
Off we go with a trip, trot, trot
Ears go flip and your tail will flop
Pony, ride and please don't stop.

Pony, pony, up I hop
We'll go a little ride to the shop
Then we'll buy some choc for me
Sugar for pony and cake for tea.

Pony, pony, up the hill
Pony, are you feeling ill
Pony, pony, down the dale
Pony, you are looking pale!

Pony, pony, quickly trot
Ride the pretty pony till he stops
Ride the pony until he drops
Ride the pony till the pony drops!

Trip, trip, trot, trip, trip, trot
Ride the pony till the pony stops!

L A Churchill

THE WISER BIRCH TREE

There lived a little Birch Tree
In the middle of a wood,
Tho' he never grew much taller,
He always wished he could.

This little Birch Tree envied
The Ash and noble Oak.
'I wish that I was big,' he said,
'To be little is no joke!'

He gazed upon the Poplar,
The Beech and Sycamore,
The Chestnut and the Lime Tree,
Who all were strong and sure.

Then the little Birch Tree heard
An almost deafening crash,
And to his great astonishment,
A Woodman had felled the Ash.

Beech and Poplar followed next,
The Woodman did not wait,
And many of the noble trees
Soon met the same sad fate.

'Oh!' cried the little Birch Tree,
As he saw the last one fall,
'If that's the fate of the mighty,
I'm thankful I am so small.'

Loré Föst

A TIDY BEDROOM

I think my bedroom's tidy
But my mum does not agree,
She says I've got to clean it up
But it looks alright to me.

The comics in the corner
Can't be thrown away,
'Cause my uncle told me
They'll be worth something one day.

There's some Lego in the corner
Which could go in its box.
But I've already filled that up
With all of my odd socks.

My drawing book and pencils
Must be kept close by.
In case I need to draw something
Like an earwig or a pie.

Here's an old crisp packet
I'll aim it for the bin,
Uh oh, here's the crisps that all fell out,
Don't think they'll go back in.

If I tidy up the comics
And shove stuff under the bed,
Bung a few things in the toy box
And some on the shelf overhead.

That should keep Mum happy
And stop her moaning for a while
'Cause I've had enough of cleaning
It just really aint my style.

Lyn Ball

DOGS AND ANIMALS

Dogs are fun
When they are on the run
Walking around
Ending up in the pound.

Animals are funny
Especially a bunny
Eating some grub
From the tub.

Catherine Shurey (10)

TEDDY BEAR

Oh teddy bear, oh teddy bear,
Why do you sit and stare
At me like that?
Eyes big, round and black,
A button nose,
Feet, but no toes,
And hands without fingers.

Helen-Elaine Oliver (13)

EEEK!

Hanging upside down by a silvery thread,
Steve the Spider lives out in the shed.
His body is black, his legs are hairy,
Some people seem to think he's scary.
Poor Steve is always hanging around,
His feet have never touched the ground.
He gets so sad in his web all day,
Wishing someone would come to play.
He counts his legs, one to eight,
And still he sits in his web to wait.

Poor Steve, he has no friends at all,
He is so lonely and very small.
'Why won't anyone come to tea?
Why is everyone afraid of me?
I won't hurt you, I do not bite,
How come I give you such a fright?
My body is black, my legs are hairy,
But I promise, I'm not scary.
I'm Steve the Spider and I live in the shed,
Hanging upside down by a silvery thread.'

Alison Thrower

SUBMISSIONS INVITED
SOMETHING FOR EVERYONE

POETRY NOW 2001 - Any subject,
any style, any time.

WOMENSWORDS 2001 - Strictly women,
have your say the female way!

STRONGWORDS 2001 - Warning!
Age restriction, must be between 16-24,
opinionated and have strong views.
(Not for the faint-hearted)

All poems no longer than 30 lines.
Always welcome! No fee!
Cash Prizes to be won!

Mark your envelope (eg *Poetry Now) 2001*
Send to:
Forward Press Ltd
Remus House, Coltsfoot Drive,
Peterborough, PE2 9JX

**OVER £10,000 POETRY PRIZES
TO BE WON!**

Judging will take place in October 2001